PRAISE FOR
HEALING FAITH

In Healing Faith, Dr. Janet Hurley offers a rare and needed gift to the healthcare community—an honest, theologically grounded exploration of spiritual warfare woven thoughtfully into the realities of modern medical practice. With clinical clarity and pastoral compassion, she illuminates how faith and science are not competitors but complementary tools for helping patients find wholeness. Her stories resonate deeply with anyone who has wrestled with complex behavioral health challenges and sensed that something more was at play. As a missionary doctor in Kenya for twenty years, I found the topic of demonic influence on patients' behavioral health status much easier to address. This book will encourage Christian clinicians to pursue excellent medicine while recognizing the profound spiritual dimensions of human suffering and healing.

—Michael E. Chupp, MD, FACS, CEO, *Christian Medical & Dental Associations*

***

I wasn't sure what to expect when I began reading Dr. Hurley's book. It didn't take long, however, to realize that she is addressing something rarely discussed—spiritual warfare. Her use of personal experiences brings the subject to life in a compelling and relatable way.

Dr. Hurley does an excellent job of honestly examining the reality that medicine is not always the complete answer. Too often, the medical profession pushes treatments into a "this pill will fix it" box. She highlights how the possibility of a spiritual attack or influence on a person's health is frequently dismissed altogether.

Having lived with a depression diagnosis for more than 50 years, I understand how this can happen. I was fortunate to have a Christian doctor and a Christian psychiatrist who looked at all treatment options and recognized that I simply needed a small dose of medication to correct a chemical imbalance.

As someone who has worked alongside pastors and church leaders in my association, I believe this is a valuable book for them to read and consider. Opening one's eyes to the possibility that Satan can influence both spiritual and physical health may help many people find the healing they desperately need.
—Dr. Danny Pickens, DedMin, Pastor/Retired Director of Missions, *Smith Baptist Association*

***

As a pastor who has conversations with people regularly about mental health, illnesses, and general problems they are facing in their lives, I am incredibly thankful that Dr. Janet Hurley has written this book to address these issues from a holistic perspective. She does a masterful job of highlighting both the benefit of medicine and the neglected truth about spiritual warfare and how our enemy is at work to steal, kill, and destroy. Through vulnerability, real-life stories, and the truth of Scripture, Dr. Hurley reveals the tactics of the enemy and how to experience victory and freedom in Christ as His beloved saints.

—**Jason White**, Lead Pastor at *Colonial Hills Baptist Church*

***

Traditionally, medical education has ignored the spiritual nature of patients, treating them as mere material beings with brain functions and emotions that often become disordered. In recent years, credentialing agencies have recognized that patients' spiritual needs, values, and beliefs should be taken into account. But what does that look like?

Dr. Janet Hurley draws upon her vast clinical knowledge, life experience, and Christian faith to craft an outline for how doctors can recognize spiritual distress in their patients and use spiritual insights to guide them toward better, and often more lasting, improvement and a state of health. I highly recommend this book for physicians and patients alike. I plan to make this book available in my office for patients to read and subsequently apply in their own lives.

—Matthew Porter, MD, FAAFP, Family Medicine & Hospice physician; *Texas Representative for American Academy of Medical Ethics*

***

Dr Hurley steps out boldly in her path of Medicine and Faith, which she does not identify as parallel paths, but as one path. In this book, she lays out temporal and Scriptural evidence for including principles of Christian faith in her role as physician. Her words reflect her life, particularly in her reliance on compassion and humility, which I have witnessed in person through years of work in the governance realm of Family Medicine. The reader can be assured that this book is not simply a collection of aspirational platitudes, but a journal from the front line of spiritual warfare.

—James A Taylor, Jr, MD, FAAFP, *Zachary, LA*

***

In Healing Faith, Dr. Janet Hurley brings together the worlds of medicine and ministry with wisdom, discernment, and courage. Drawing on years of family practice and practical family experience, she shares how professionals and laymen alike can search below the surface of people's mental, physical and spiritual challenges and explore the possibility that there is something deeper going on in our lives. Her stories of spiritual warfare are deeply personal, vulnerable and extraordinary, and each point to a solution for our pain that is redemptive, practical and powerful. Healing Faith will challenge your thinking, encourage your faith, and remind you of the power of the "Big H" over the "little d."

—**Michael Curtis,** Certified Master of the Leadership Challenge©, Director, *Three Strands Marriage Ministry*

***

I believe Healing Faith achieves the goal the writer, Dr Janet Hurley, desires, addressing in detail various attempts by the evil one to take control of our lives and ways to recognize and spoil Satan's attempts.

The book is unique in that it is written through the eyes of a physician, especially a fellow family physician. Dr. Janet Hurley's book is not just another book on spiritual warfare; Healing Faith includes very practical and potentially afterlife-saving lessons in the form of a reference text learned from decades of patient encounters as a physician colleague literally working "in the trenches" of a general medicine practice.

The book is an extraordinary story written through a mother, wife, daughter, and physician's perspective of her own personal faith story. It should be a must-read for any healthcare worker, particularly medical students and residents."

—Wayne Gravois, MD, *Baton Rouge, LA*

Healing Faith

Empowering Wellness Through Spiritual Warfare

Janet L. Hurley, MD

Published by KHARIS PUBLISHING,
an imprint of KHARIS MEDIA LLC.

ISBN-13: 978-1-63746-690-2

ISBN-10: 1-63746-690-0

Library of Congress Control Number: 2026935261

All KHARIS PUBLISHING products are available at special quantity discounts for bulk purchases for sales promotions, premiums, fund-raising, and educational needs. For details, contact:

Kharis Media LLC
Tel: +1 (331) 312-2376
support@kharispublishing.com
www.kharispublishing.com

DEDICATION

To my daughter, Alyssa, who bravely allowed me to share her story and designed the book cover.

To my husband, Dennis, and my son, Kaden, who also supported me through this process.

To Jennifer Jones, who opened our eyes to spiritual warfare under our own roof. May all people in bondage be blessed with a "Jennifer Jones" to speak boldly despite skepticism.

To Michael Curtis, my first editor, encourager, and friend.

To my church family at Colonial Hills Baptist Church, which has stayed grounded in the grace message under the shepherding of Robert Carter and Jason White. My church will always have a place on the pew for you!

Special thanks to Kharis Publishing for giving this new author a chance and guiding me along the way.

And to my patients whose stories are told in this book, for they are what make it worth reading.

NOTE: Patient names have been changed to protect patient privacy.

TABLE OF CONTENTS

PROLOGUE

After 20 years of practicing clinical primary care medicine, I've learned there are behavioral and emotional problems that medication alone cannot fix. Working in an area with limited access to psychiatrists often requires me to manage a higher number of patients with depression, anxiety, and other behavioral health conditions. Yet beyond mental health conditions, I have treated many chronic diseases resulting from poor lifestyle habits that patients find difficult to change. They *know* what they should do, but do not do it. They *want* to change, but they don't. All too often, we overlook the spiritual factors influencing patients' healthcare decisions, therefore missing the opportunity to help them navigate through it.

While some individuals with depression and anxiety due to biochemical brain imbalances respond well to medication, others do not. For these patients, we often try one drug after another, sometimes combining multiple medications, and refer them to different counselors. Yet, for some, nothing seems to work. Many of these patients have spent their lives trapped by false beliefs about themselves or the world around them that no medication can resolve.

Over time, I've come to understand that, for some people, the true battle lies in the mind—not in the physical brain, but in the thinking part of our soul that shapes who we are as individuals. I've also realized that spiritual warfare is real, yet most people don't recognize it or know how to confront it.

If you are a physician who has felt despondent about difficult patients for whom traditional medicine does not seem to work, this book will offer you another treatment for your toolbox. If you are a patient striving to sleep better, eat well, and exercise, yet find yourself sabotaged by intrusive thoughts and entrenched habits, this book lights a path forward. Stop beating yourself up for your failures and put the blame on the evil forces where it actually belongs. Then stand firm against them.

This book shares real stories, with names changed to protect patient privacy, that illuminate the problems and offer credible, compassionate solutions. My hope is that these "victory stories" will kindle hope and healing, allowing light to emerge from the torment these individuals endured. Their triumphs can be yours, too.

Victory begins with recognizing spiritual attacks in real time and responding by standing firm in truth. That is the focus of this book.

I

Defining the Problem

CHAPTER 1

DEFINING THE PROBLEM

I did not begin my medical career believing in spiritual warfare, nor did I start my Christian walk with that belief. I taught Sunday School for years and was dedicated to attending a grace-based church that emphasized freedom in Christ. Yet somehow, I overlooked the role spiritual warfare plays in people's lives.

Then one day, it became undeniable—in a dramatic way—when my daughter was 12 years old. We knew she had an underlying anxiety disorder, and the medications she began taking at age seven brought rapid and remarkable improvement that lasted for years. Yet in junior high, things started to change. She became more anxious, more frustrated, and more secretive. She started eating lunch with a different group of kids at school who would turn over papers and hide things whenever parents came to visit. Something was wrong, but I couldn't see it, even though it was right in front of me.

Her behavior was attributed to worsening anxiety, hormonal changes, bad influences, and poor decisions.

My husband and I responded with thoughtful counsel and appropriate discipline, but nothing seemed to work.

She was sent to a counselor, but he couldn't identify the problem. She wasn't bullied at school. She wasn't experiencing abuse. There were no financial or marital stressors at home, nor had the family suffered any recent losses. What were we missing?

At one point, she had a severe panic attack and asked to speak with her youth pastor. The meeting was quickly arranged. The primary issue, it seemed, was her need for reassurance about her salvation. Our faith teaches the doctrine that Jesus paid the penalty for all sin and defeated both sin and death on the cross. Once someone accepts Christ as their Savior, that person is saved forever. She had never been taught that salvation could be lost, so where had she gotten that idea?

At a youth retreat one weekend, she had another panic attack. During the second evening, one of the adult youth leaders brought up the topic of spiritual warfare. To be honest, I had no idea what she was talking about. I listened politely and responded with a "dose of doctor"—explaining anxiety, neurotransmitters, and the child's poor choice of friends.

"Would you read a book for me?" the leader asked as our conversation was winding down. I agreed. After all, I'd spent years in school; surely, I could read a book. But what I read in those pages transformed my perspective forever.

The book was *The Bondage Breaker* by Dr. Neil Anderson. He wrote about his years as a Christian counselor and how, initially, he didn't fully grasp the reality and impact of spiritual warfare. This lack of understanding limited his effectiveness with certain patients. Dr. Anderson described a "two-tiered worldview" prevalent in our culture, where spiritual forces and the physical world are seen as separate and unrelated. However, he provided scriptural evidence showing that these realms are deeply interconnected. By the time I finished Chapter 2, I realized I had missed the spiritual warfare taking place in my very own home, under my own roof, in my daughter's bedroom.

I've asked many people how they would respond if they came home to find an intruder attacking someone they loved. Most describe feelings of fierce protection and a willingness to fight back. None suggested blaming their loved one for being upset or anxious—such a response would be unthinkable. Yet what if the enemy was in your home, but invisible to you? What if we had "magic glasses" that allowed us to see the spiritual forces at work around us? How would that change our responses to alcoholics, habitual liars, or those struggling with mental illness?

What if we could see the torment they endure from unseen spiritual forces? If we are the ones struggling, how would this change our perspective of ourselves?

For the first time in months, my husband and I found ourselves finally on our daughter's side. We stopped criticizing her behavior, realizing we had unknowingly been playing into the enemy's hands. Yet we still didn't know how to confront an invisible foe. We had to set aside our usual methods of discipline and adopt a new kind of warfare. Ephesians 4:27 warns us not to give the devil a foothold through sin, but we didn't know what foothold he was using with our daughter.

Then one evening, my husband discovered the answer. My daughter, with her love of science and natural curiosity about her changing body, had come across graphic medical images. Though we had set safe search filters on all our devices, she still stumbled upon content that made her feel ashamed. But who had told her to feel ashamed? And when she turned away, who urged her to look again? That "who" had a name: the devil and his demons.

While we didn't yet know how to wage spiritual warfare, we decided to have a family meeting to confront her about what we had found on her tablet. The conversation didn't start well, and our daughter became defensive. But then, the Holy Spirit led my husband to change his approach entirely. He apologized to her for allowing this to happen. "I am your father, and I'm supposed to protect you from this. Will you forgive me?" In that moment, my daughter melted into his arms. Her entire demeanor changed, and she willingly handed over her devices with relief.

The transformation was striking. In just 20 minutes, the devil's grip of guilt and shame on our daughter was broken. My husband took that guilt onto himself, and in doing so, we saw our daughter freed. I wish I could fully convey the remarkable change we witnessed in those brief moments. The enemy was utterly defeated, and we had our daughter back.

Many people with mental illness need medication. My daughter, who has biochemical anxiety, benefits greatly from medicine. But at age 12, her problem was neither medical nor biochemical. Her problem was spiritual, and we had missed it for months.

As we followed standard discipline techniques with verbal instruction and removal of privileges, we unintentionally stoked her anxiety further and played even more into the devil's hand. Unknowingly, we were attacking the victim.

CHAPTER 2

PRACTICING MEDICINE THROUGH A NEW LENS

I am quick to remind my patients that I am their doctor, not their pastor. I understand how vulnerable people can be in times of need, and basic medical ethics does not permit me to impose my faith on those who do not want it. However, I live in a community with a significant number of Christians who believe that Jesus is the Messiah and that He came to pay the penalty for our sins. With many of my patients, our worldviews align. My community is small enough that I know some of my patients very well.

One such patient, whom I will call Jane, transferred to my practice during her mid-childhood. She had been diagnosed with ADHD and responded well to medication for years. But as she transitioned into her preteen years, things began to change. She became significantly more anxious and depressed. Despite trying different medications and counseling, there was no meaningful improvement.

Jane turned to reading as a way to escape. While this kept her out of trouble, it also distracted her from chores and responsibilities, which caused tension between her and her parents. She began overeating and gained considerable weight. Her parents, concerned about her health, tried to control her eating, but Jane started sneaking food at night. The family's frustrations escalated to the point where her parents considered sending her to a boarding school for a time.

At one follow-up visit, Jane was still very depressed and mentioned hearing voices telling her she was worthless. I started her on an antipsychotic, but it didn't help. I referred her to a psychiatrist.

When Jane saw the psychiatrist, he asked detailed questions about the voices: Did she hear them inside or outside her head? Were they in one ear or the other? Was it a male or female voice? At the end of the evaluation, the psychiatrist concluded that she was making it up. Jane's father, who was present during the visit, left believing his daughter was a liar. Their relationship deteriorated further, and Jane, feeling unheard and invalidated, developed maladaptive coping mechanisms. She learned to say what others wanted to hear, claiming the voices were gone when, in reality, they were not.

When Jane was almost 18 years old, she aged out of the pediatric psychiatry practice and returned to me for her behavioral health care. At that visit, it became clear that her condition had not improved during the six years under psychiatric care. Yet unlike six years earlier, I now had an understanding of spiritual warfare.

Seeing her case with fresh eyes, I realized I had failed her. With her and her parents' blessing, I transferred her medical care to my partner, stepped down as her doctor, and took on the role of her mentor instead.

Jane and I met weekly for several months, working through the youth edition of *The Bondage Breaker* one chapter at a time. Her relationship with her parents steadily improved. She graduated from high school and has maintained full-time employment ever since. She now drives and has held the same job for over eight years.

Eventually, Jane weaned herself off all her medications, and her depression has remained in remission. I believe she still has biochemical ADHD, but now that she is out of school, medication is less critical. Looking back, I am convinced that much of her anxiety and depression stemmed from spiritual warfare.

I believe that once a person is saved, the Holy Spirit comes to dwell within them. When this happens, a person cannot be possessed by a demon. However, one can still be influenced by them. The devil often speaks to us in our own voice, in the first person, as if it's our own thoughts. While some individuals may experience biological psychosis due to conditions like depression, schizophrenia, or other psychiatric disorders, not everyone who hears voices is psychotic. Jane felt an immense sense of relief when she realized she could be honest with me about the voices. She knew I would believe her and help her stand firm against them.

I can only imagine how much better her life could have been if we had identified the real problem earlier—or how much worse it might have been if we had never discovered it at all.

CHAPTER 3

THE DANGER OF LONG-TERM BONDAGE

I had another patient in my practice whom I will call George. George had sustained multiple war injuries during his young adult years, leaving him with chronic pain. Despite this, he was hesitant to take medications or pursue advanced treatments.

George also lived with significant anxiety for much of his life, yet he managed to cope well during his working years. His anxiety was visibly intense—he would pace the floor and fidget during every office visit. Time and again, I explained the medication options available for his pain and anxiety, but he consistently declined. Knowing that my usual approach wasn't working, I decided one day to try something different.

As I've mentioned before, I am not my patients' preacher, but I often explore what other tools might help them. For instance, understanding support systems—whether family, friends, or a church—can make a significant difference. That day, I asked George about his spiritual life. He shared that he and his wife had faithfully attended a Christian church for many years. But then, he hesitated and said, "…but I know God could never want me." That "mic drop" moment made it clear to me that my schedule that day was about to fall behind. For the first time in years, I was able to see the spiritual assault he was under.

"What do you mean, God could never want you?" I asked. What George shared next left me deeply grieved.

During the war, his unit's actions led to tragedy. During an enemy engagement, one of the enemies they had shot was holding a child. George felt personally responsible for the child's death and had carried the weight of that guilt for decades.

Was it possible that George avoided advanced treatments for his pain and anxiety because he believed he deserved to suffer? It's unlikely anyone in the military, his family, or his friends told him such things. So where did this belief come from? And who had been feeding him these condemning thoughts all these years? To ignore the spiritual forces at work in George's life would have been to deny him the only thing that could set him free.

I asked him what his pastor had taught about the purpose of Jesus' ministry on Earth. Did Jesus come to pay the penalty for all of humanity's sins, "or for everyone else's sin but yours?" I reminded him of

Paul's words: *"For our struggle is not against flesh and blood, but against the rulers, against the authorities, against the powers of this dark world and against the spiritual forces of evil in the heavenly realms"* (Eph. 6:12).

As Neil Anderson writes in *The Bondage Breaker*, battles with demons are not power encounters—they are truth encounters. At that moment, the main thing George needed was a dose of truth.

I eventually lost contact with George over the years, but one of our final interactions was his thank-you message. He expressed gratitude that I cared not only about my patients' physical needs but also their spiritual needs. I later learned that he had shared *The Bondage Breaker* with several of his friends.

I would like to believe George is free, but I know how difficult it can be to untangle decades of torment and the maladaptive coping behaviors that often follow. Bill Gillham discusses these ingrained patterns of behavior in his book *Lifetime Guarantee*. He describes them as "green superhighways" programmed into our brains in response to specific stimuli. Similarly, Dr. Jeffrey Schwartz and Dr. Rebecca Gladding, psychiatrists, write in *You Are Not Your Brain* about how our brains physically adapt by forming and reinforcing neural connections. They explain that while these pathways can be rewired, it requires focused effort and time. One point made clear in their is, *"The power is in the focus!"*

For example, if someone is right-handed and breaks their right arm, they will temporarily rely on their left hand. Over time, their brain learns the most efficient neural pathways for completing tasks with the left hand. However, once the cast is removed, the person will naturally favor their right hand again, as those pathways are more deeply ingrained. If someone were to permanently lose their right hand, the brain would continue refining its left-hand pathways, improving its efficiency over time.

I believe a similar process occurs with spiritual struggles. People often use negative coping strategies for years to deal with spiritual battles. As Gillham points out, we don't have a "reset" button. Even after someone becomes a believer, they must unlearn the maladaptive behaviors on which they previously relied. They must consistently focus on truth for days, months, and sometimes years. For Christians, salvation frees us from the power of sin, but we must still fight daily against negative thoughts and behaviors ingrained in our minds. George had decades of programming to undo, and that kind of transformation doesn't happen overnight.

We cannot sever these spiritual wounds from our bodies entirely. We must continue to focus on truth day after day, and over time, the brain will start to "ignore" the old pathways in favor of the new ones.

Our goal should be to recognize and address spiritual bondage as early as possible, just as the youth worker did for my daughter. Unfortunately, many Christians don't know the basics of spiritual warfare or the tactics used by the enemy. All too often, the enemy is present, and we don't even realize it.

II

The Modalities of Attack

CHAPTER 4

DECEPTION—
"I'M NOT REALLY HERE"

If someone were to say something harsh to you while standing right in front of you, you'd have a choice at that moment to believe them or not. But what if the mean, critical voice you hear is in your head, spoken in your own voice, and phrased in the first person? What if some of the thoughts you hear aren't really from you?

Scripture describes the fruit of the Spirit in Galatians 5:22–23: "love, joy, peace, patience, kindness, goodness, faithfulness, gentleness, and self-control." So, what should we think about emotions that oppose these virtues? When we feel anger, jealousy, or offense, where do these emotions come from? Perhaps they stem from old, ingrained patterns in our brains, as described by Bill Gillham. However, it's also possible they originate from spiritual forces speaking to us *as if they were us*—in our own voice and perspective. Unfortunately, many Christians struggle to discern the difference.

For example, if you argue with a family member because you've had a bad day, the Holy Spirit will likely prompt you later to reach out to your loved one to seek repentance and reconciliation. The Spirit's coaching is often specific: *"Earlier today, when you spoke harshly to your mom on the phone, that was rude."* This specificity encourages an apology and restoration. In contrast, the enemy's voice is vague and accusatory. Instead of addressing a specific action, it whispers lies like, *"I am a bad son/daughter,"* or, *"I am a bad Christian."* These generalized accusations are not from God.

All people fail. Christians fail. Some Christians fail often. But if you've recently had a major moral failure, it's worth considering whether the enemy was involved. The enemy is opportunistic—he attacks when we're down, preys on our weaknesses, and seeks to sabotage our fruitfulness for Christ. The enemy wants to convince us that the problem is entirely within ourselves.

One of the hallmarks of deception is that the person does not know they are being deceived. The enemy often deceives us into believing the problem is our parents, our situation, the person we married, the church we attend, or some other outside influence. It is only when we recognize the deception and see the enemy at play that we can start fighting the deception with truth.

In *The Bondage Breaker,* Neil Anderson explains deception like this: "If I deceived you, you wouldn't know it. If you knew you were being deceived, then you would no longer be deceived." This is the crux of the problem. If you continue believing that the issue is solely you— or your parents, your spouse, your boss, your church, or some other person—the enemy will maintain his hold.

Let me clarify: I am not talking about demon possession. Once someone receives the Holy Spirit, that person cannot then be possessed by a demon. However, Christians can still be influenced by demonic forces. Why else would Paul instruct us in Ephesians to "put on the full armor of God" and "take up the shield of faith, with which you can extinguish all the flaming arrows of the evil one" (Eph. 6:13a, 16)? While we are immune to possession, we are not immune to spiritual attack.

I had a patient who suffered from severe anxiety and night terrors. She would often wake up crying, and only tranquilizers or an embrace would bring relief. We tried various traditional anti-anxiety medications, but none had been effective. Her caregiver, strong in the faith, did not believe spiritual forces could be involved. But what if he was deceived? And if he was deceived, how would he even know? If she understood that these fearful thoughts might be coming from the enemy and realized that she has the same authority as Jesus Christ to command the enemy to flee, how might this transform her situation?

The devil thrives in the shadows. He wants you to believe he isn't there, that the problem is entirely you, and that spiritual warfare doesn't exist.

C.S. Lewis offers an insightful perspective in his classic book, *The Screwtape Letters*. In this fictional work, a junior demon is assigned to influence a person and receives guidance from a senior demon. Initially, the demon's goal is to prevent the individual from being saved. Once the person becomes a Christian, the demon's focus shifts to keeping them so distracted and busy that they cannot bear fruit for Christ.

While Lewis's work is fictional, it paints a compelling picture of spiritual warfare. Though Christians cannot be demon-possessed, we can be demon-influenced. The devil cannot steal our salvation, but he can render us ineffective.

If you are willing to consider that spiritual warfare is real, you might now feel afraid. But take heart—the devil can only influence you if you permit him. When Jesus rose on the third day, the devil was defeated. He no longer has authority over you. When the Holy Spirit entered your life, you received the same authority over demons that Jesus Himself had. The problem is that many of us don't know how to wield this authority. Worse, we may not even realize we need to start.

The devil's ultimate goal is to convince you he isn't there. He wants you to stop reading this, to dismiss the idea of spiritual warfare entirely. He may have lost your soul, but he's determined to keep you from bearing fruit for Christ. If deception can't work, then he will surely tempt you. After all, don't you deserve better?

CHAPTER 5

TEMPTATION— "YOU DESERVE BETTER"

Submission does not come naturally to me. When I was growing up, my parents were divorced, my mom relied on welfare, and we survived on food stamps and government-issued cheese. Climbing out of that situation required intense focus and persistence. Along the way, I developed certain beliefs that later caused struggles: I believed education could take me anywhere, that science could explain everything, and that I was in charge of my own destiny.

As I grew older and faced infertility, my trust in science and education eroded and I was left searching for something greater. This struggle ultimately led to my salvation, as my stubborn heart came to realize I was *not* in charge of my destiny. There is a God who is bigger than me, and His plans are far greater than mine. God withheld something I deeply desired to bring me to the end of myself and toward Him.

This world glorifies self-sufficiency, self-reward, and self-satisfaction. It promotes the mindset of *"What's in it for me?"* Even acts of apparent selflessness are often done for recognition. Names are etched onto buildings, plaques, and park benches to commemorate generosity. Yet, these same individuals eventually end up in the grave, their bodies returning to dust like everyone else. The only thing we can take with us to heaven is people—the souls of those we influence along the way. Our riches, possessions, and earthly achievements mean nothing to our eternal souls. Yet we continue to yearn for, hunger after, and chase things that hold no eternal value.

Paul warns us in 1 Timothy 6:10 that it isn't money itself but the *love of money* that leads to trouble. God doesn't call all of us to sell everything and become missionaries, but He does call each of us to submit to the specific plan He has for our lives. We either choose to submit or we don't. Paul also writes in Philippians 4:12, "I have learned the secret of being content in any and every situation, whether well fed or hungry, whether living in plenty or in want." True contentment is the foundation of spiritual peace. Yet we often continue chasing after things that are temporary, meaningless, and sometimes even harmful.

The devil wants us to believe that there's always something more—something God is withholding. Just as he deceived Adam and Eve in the Garden of Eden, he whispers lies that we can be like God, that we know what's best for our lives, and that we can control our own destiny. These are all lies. And if we continue to listen to that garbage, we will fall prey to the same deception that Adam and Eve faced in the garden.

The enemy tempts us with food, possessions, and sensations. He appeals to the lust of our eyes and the desires of our flesh (1 John 2:16). He manipulates our pride, making us feel entitled to pleasure, acceptance, and material gain. Yet, even as the devil tempts us, God desires to give us good things and promises to provide for our needs (Philippians 4:19). He knows what is good for us and sets things in motion to provide it.

I have met people who radiate spiritual peace, the kind of peace for which we all have a deep longing. Some have many possessions, while others have very few. True joy doesn't come from material wealth but from the spiritual peace that arises when we trust and accept God's plan for our lives. The alternative is a life of anger and despair.

When we read the Psalms, we see King David pouring out his heart to God in moments of deep despair. Yet he consistently reminds himself of God's past faithfulness and praises Him for His wondrous works. Reflecting on the beauty of God's creation—the wind and the rain, the mountains and the seas—can lead to profound gratitude and a deeper trust in Him. This trust brings the spiritual peace we all crave, a peace we will never find in a bottle, an indulgent meal, or an expensive home.

When my grandfather was 97 years old and still in good health, I asked him if he had a "bucket list" of things he wanted to accomplish. His response surprised me. He said he didn't have one—he was "perfectly content." Initially, I felt disappointed, thinking there was nothing I could do to show my love for him. But then I realized I should aspire to be more like him—truly content.

The devil will try to convince you that there's satisfaction beyond what God can provide. In doing so, he entices us to believe we can be our own gods. Nothing could be further from the truth. When this happens, we should exercise our "faith muscle" and use the temptation as an opportunity to grow.

In his book, *The Bondage Breaker*, Neil Anderson provides a vivid illustration: Imagine yourself as a Christian walking down an alley lined with two-story apartment complexes. Jesus is waiting for you at the end of the road, and the devil and his demons are trapped behind the windows of those buildings. Since the devil is a defeated foe, he cannot touch you—his only weapon is enticement.

Some Christians become infatuated with the things they see in the windows and lose focus, diminishing their ability to witness for Christ. Others become consumed with anger toward the devil, wasting time shouting at him and fighting battles that Jesus has already won. In both cases, the devil succeeds in making them ineffective.

Then there are Christians who break away from the distractions and refocus on their journey toward

God. But when the devil sees their victory, he switches tactics to condemnation. He whispers lies meant to paralyze them with despair: *"You're no good."* His goal is to make even a victorious Christian sit down in the middle of the road, believing they are unworthy. And when they are stuck sitting in the middle of the road, they cannot bear as much fruit for Christ.

During the rest of this book, we will refer to this walk towards Jesus as "the Christian walk."

Chapter 6

Condemnation—"You Are No Good"

It is a profound gift to have a forgiving God. God sent His Son to die for us, paying the penalty for the sins of the world. It's difficult to comprehend how He could love us so deeply. I remember holding my first child in my arms, overwhelmed by the love I felt. In that moment, I was reminded that God loves me even more than I love my own child.

My son was born three days after Christmas, and after his birth, the Christmas song *"Mary, Did You Know?"* resonated with me on a whole new level. Mary, did you know that Jesus is God's Son? Did you know He would understand Scripture better than you as a young child? Did you know He would endure ruthless torture and be sacrificed for the sins of the world? Did you know He would experience separation from God in the agony of hell before rising again to redeem humanity?

Too often, Christians today forget these foundational truths, and the devil uses that forgetfulness to his advantage.

I once had a patient who struggled with alcoholism for years. I worked with his family to detox him at home, prescribing medications and providing detailed instructions for his care. I also treated his underlying depression and regularly followed up with him as he maintained sobriety. Unfortunately, he eventually relapsed, stopped coming to the clinic, and fell back into his addiction.

One day, he was hospitalized after falling while intoxicated. His time in the hospital detoxed his body, and he returned to my office after being discharged. I will never forget what he said: *"I hated coming back here because I knew you would be so disappointed in me."*

In reality, I was thrilled he had returned to sobriety and sought help again. I wasn't disappointed—I was hopeful. But I couldn't help wondering: *Who* told him I would be disappointed? Where did he get that idea?

I reassured him that I wasn't disappointed but excited for the fresh opportunity we had to work together on his recovery. I celebrated his survival of the accident, his sobriety in the weeks following his hospitalization, and his decision to seek help again. These were victories worth acknowledging! So, who planted the idea that I would condemn him? That "who" has a name: Satan.

This patient was part of a local Christian church, so I reminded him of a vital truth—he had an enemy.

The enemy whispered lies to isolate him, convincing him that I was disappointed, that I couldn't help, or that he wasn't strong enough to overcome his addiction. Sadly, these condemning thoughts continued to haunt him, and he died far too young.

We all make mistakes. We lose our temper, say things we regret, or make careless errors like backing into a car. We may stumble onto things online we know we shouldn't see or revert to harmful habits in an attempt to meet perceived "needs." But none of this means we lose our salvation. None of this means God is through with us or that we are useless in His kingdom.

My former pastor, Robert Carter, often quoted Adrian Rogers, who said, *"Does it ever occur to you that nothing ever occurs to God?"* It is often said that nothing ever surprises God. God is never shocked or caught off guard by our actions. He knows the beginning and the end. He sees the entire tapestry of our lives and knows exactly what to do to steer us in the right direction.

Life is messy. People are messy. Relationships are messy. But none of this makes us useless to God.

The devil, however, wants you to believe otherwise. He tells you that you're a "bad Christian" and that you can't do anything meaningful for Christ. His goal is to make you sit down in the middle of your

Christian walk, bearing no fruit for God's kingdom. While he has already lost your soul, he will do everything he can to rob you of your daily victory.

No Christian has an excuse to stop bearing fruit for Christ. For some, bearing fruit might look like preaching in large arenas. For others, it might mean volunteering at a nursing home, mentoring children, donating generously, or helping clean up after ministry events. Every role is valuable, and every gift has a purpose.

In Matthew 25, Jesus tells the Parable of the Talents. One servant was given five talents and doubled them through wise investments. Another servant, given two talents, also doubled his. But the servant given one talent buried it in the ground, returning only what he was initially given. He was reprimanded for failing to use it wisely. None of us should bury our talents.

Sadly, many Christians today are like the servant who buried his talent. They sit down in the middle of the road, weighed down by the devil's condemnation. They feel useless, stop attending church, neglect prayer and Bible study, and stagnate spiritually. Meanwhile, the devil looks on with satisfaction.

But there is a better way. We don't have to succumb to these lies. We can stand firm, walk forward, and live the fruitful lives God has called us to. We simply need to learn how.

III

The Way Out

CHAPTER 7

THE HOOKS THAT KEEP US STUCK

Do you ever wonder why you find yourself caught in a cycle of sin, confession, and repentance—only to repeat the same sin again? Why didn't confession solve the problem? Why didn't repentance lead to lasting change?

Many Christians mistakenly believe they're trapped in a cosmic tug-of-war, with God pulling them one way and the devil pulling them the other. But that is one of the devil's biggest lies! When God sent His Son to defeat sin and death, the devil became a defeated foe. Scripture tells us, "After disarming the powers and authorities, He made a public spectacle of them" (Colossians 2:15). God triumphed, displaying His might and glory, crushing the devil like an insect.

Here's the remarkable part: Romans 8:11 reminds us that the same power that raised Jesus from the dead lives in us! When you are born again and the Holy Spirit indwells you, you are given the authority of Jesus Himself in spiritual matters. Yet, despite this incredible truth, we still fall into sin. Why is that?

At its core, most sin stems from unbelief. We doubt that God is strong enough to meet our needs. We don't believe we have the strength to overcome addiction. We convince ourselves that our biology or circumstances render us powerless. But if the Creator of the universe, who defeated sin and death, dwells within us, we already have all the power we need. We just need to believe it.

Neil Anderson's "Steps to Freedom in Christ" helps readers identify key hooks the enemy has used in their lives. Three I wish to highlight are unforgiveness, guilt, and pride.

Unforgiveness

Much has been written, sung, and preached about forgiveness. Beneath these messages often lies an earthly desire for justice. I watched bitterness destroy my father. Decades ago, his brother was stabbed to death. The incident was ruled self-defense, and no charges were filed. My father's unforgiveness turned into a deep anger that poisoned his ability to experience true joy. It led him down a path of addiction and cynicism.

There is a well-known saying: "Bitterness is the poison we drink, hoping it will kill someone else." This was true for my father.

Matthew West beautifully captures this idea in his song "Forgiveness," which tells the powerful story of a mother whose daughter was killed in a car accident caused by a drunk driver. Struggling with overwhelming grief and bitterness, the mother made the courageous choice to forgive the driver and even advocated for leniency in his sentencing. Together, they shared their story, turning a heartbreaking tragedy into a profound message of grace.

Another remarkable outcome of this story is that the rest of the family also forgave the driver. Their story has since been shared in numerous venues, inspiring countless others. The driver, a young man in his twenties at the time of the accident, developed a close relationship with the family. The mother once said she lost a daughter but gained a son. This is the transformative power of forgiveness.

Forgiveness is not a suggestion; it's a command. In the *Parable of the Unmerciful Servant* (Matthew 18:21–35), Jesus tells us to forgive "seventy times seven." True forgiveness is without conditions—what I call "forgiveness with no buts." If you think, *I forgive you, but you need to say sorry,* or *I forgive you, but you need to pay for it,* then it's not true forgiveness. While societal justice may demand consequences, in our hearts, we must release the debt completely.

God's forgiveness toward us comes with no strings attached, and we are called to extend that same grace to others—even when the relationship cannot continue or boundaries are needed to prevent harm.

Forgiveness does not mean tolerating abuse or remaining in harmful situations; sometimes, ending the relationship is necessary. Yet, in our hearts, forgiveness should always prevail. I regularly thank God that His forgiveness of me came without conditions or strings attached.

In *Victory of Darkness,* Neil Anderson clarifies: "People are not in bondage to past traumas. They are in bondage to the lies they believed about themselves, God, and how to live as a result of the past trauma." He reminds us that forgiveness is required by God and is necessary to avoid entrapment by Satan. We also need to do so if we wish to be like Christ. "You don't heal in order to forgive. You forgive in order to heal."

Forgiveness can be a process, but we have the power of God within us to enable it. Holding onto bitterness only gives the devil a foothold (Ephesians 4:27). Dr. Bruce and Toni Hebel's *Forgiving Forward* provides practical steps to uproot unforgiveness, emphasizing gratitude for God's forgiveness, repentance, and blessing those who hurt us. Though the pain may not disappear instantly, forgiveness allows us to move forward without being enslaved by anger or bitterness.

Many say that they just can't help it! They're so angry or so hurt, and they don't know how to replace those bitter thoughts with positive ones. Sometimes forgiveness is a process, yet we must begin. And we should always remember that we have the power of God living in us, which provides an eternal source of love and forgiveness that is more than we could ever need. To believe the opposite is to be deceived by the enemy. To feel the opposite will lead to the same bitter adulthood my father experienced for decades.

In this book, the Hebels provide practical steps known as "The 7 Protocols of Forgiveness." This resource is invaluable for helping people break free from the poison of unforgiveness. The process begins by thanking God for our own forgiveness, repenting of our unforgiveness, and actively forgiving each offense from the heart. To seal this decision, we should ask for God's blessing on those who have hurt us and commit to remembering their sins no more.

While this doesn't necessarily erase all the pain or undo the way past hurts have shaped our lives, it allows us to move forward, no longer letting anger 'give the devil a foothold' in our lives (Ephesians 4:27). The Hebels remind us that "bitterness is to a heart wound what infection is to a flesh wound" (Hebel & Hebel, 2011). Regardless of who caused the wound, it is the responsibility of the wounded to take the necessary steps toward healing.

Unforgiveness often distorts our perception of present reality, keeping us stuck in a cycle of pain. The Hebels challenge us with this powerful truth: "When we do not forgive, we are saying that Jesus' death may satisfy God, but it doesn't satisfy us." To refuse forgiveness is to undervalue the blood of Jesus compared to how the Father esteems it.

Their approach to forgiveness emphasizes a heart-level process that begins with gratitude for God's forgiveness and honest repentance for our own unforgiveness. They encourage people to ask God whom they need to forgive and why, then walk through each offense intentionally—releasing the debt to God and choosing forgiveness from the heart.

The process includes blessing the person forgiven, committing not to revisit the offense, and responding to painful memories with reminders of the forgiveness already given, gratitude for the freedom it brought, and renewed blessing toward the offender. Reconciliation is prayed for when appropriate. Ultimately, they call believers to make forgiveness a continual lifestyle, not a one-time event. They have a free forgiveness guide and other resources on their website, forgivingforward.com.

One of my former patients, John Crawford Wills II, courageously authored a book titled *Blessings Through the Seasons*, a collection of weekly devotionals spanning an entire year. In it, he bravely told his deepest secret of being molested at age nine by a man who picked him up at a ballpark. He never told anyone about this man, and he lived in fear of him for 45 years. But then, at age 54, he came across him one day at a local gas station. His initial response was fear, but then he saw this person had become a small, frail, old man. When they exchanged introductions, he told this man "I am that little boy you picked up from the baseball field and sexually abused in the summer of 1968!" He goes on to say:

> *His legs started to buckle, he began to shake, and asked me my name. I told him, "My name is Johnny," and began to give details. He never denied any of it. But he did ask me something that I found interesting.*
>
> *He said, "Are you going to beat me up?" I responded, "No sir. That is not why I want to talk to you. I just want to know if you will accept what I am about to say to you."*
>
> *And then I was able to do what I needed to do. I did something that day, by God's grace, which changed my life. I reached out with my right hand, took his feeble old hand, and said three words that changed my life forever: "I forgive you." And in that moment, the power of God changed my life, and set me free.*
>
> *I let it all go. Any fear, any hatred, any despair, any lack of forgiveness, any loss of hope, any lack of compassion for him, died! It simply vanished, and I was never the same. I want you to know this, and please hear me—forgiveness is an aspect of love, and love is a gift from God. If what happened to me happened to you, God can heal you.*

Mr. Wills was tall and stocky, a man who could have easily been a physical threat to the abuser from his past. However, true freedom from his pain did not come through physical confrontation but through the power of his heart. He broke free from the fear and anxiety of his past trauma through the transformative healing of forgiveness.

Without question, unforgiveness robs us of joy. And when we do not forgive ourselves, we run into another one of Satan's tactics—guilt.

Guilt

Guilt flows from unforgiveness because this usually means we have not forgiven ourselves. Yet guilt is so powerful a weapon from the enemy that it requires its own section. While it is true that no one in the church is perfect—not pastors, not leaders, and certainly not us-God does not demand perfection.

Dan Stone and David Gregory said it well in *The Rest of the Gospel*—"You are not a liability to God. You are his precious assets." 1 Corinthians 4:7 tells us "...We have this treasure in jars of clay to show that this all-surpassing power is from God and not from us." None of us is perfect; we are all cracked pots. But God uses that imperfection for his glory. It is true that we were sinners saved by grace, but once we are saved we become saints. At times, the saints sin, but that does not change their standing with God.

There are also times when we did not do anything wrong, but the enemy will make us think we did.

I once had a patient in her mid-sixties come in for a routine follow-up visit. During our conversation, I learned that she had recently taken legal custody of her 18-month-old great-grandchild. While I've known many grandparents to step in and raise their grandchildren, having a great-grandparent take on this role is far less common. Though I wasn't sure why other family members were not chosen, the courts had decided that this great-grandmother was the best choice to care for the child.

My patient seemed well-adjusted to her new role at first, but when I commended her for so selflessly dedicating her twilight years to raising a child, her demeanor changed. Despite being a hero for stepping up to care for this child, she carried a sense of guilt about the situation.

She felt responsible for her granddaughter's grief from losing custody of her child. She felt remorse for being chosen by the court over her daughter to raise the child. Deep down, she knew the child was much safer in her care, yet she struggled with guilt for being the one to make that a reality. I could sense the enemy's influence in her life, twisting her grief into guilt, trying to convince her she had done something wrong.

It is natural to feel sadness in a situation like this. She gave up so much, and her granddaughter lost so much. She sacrificed a comfortable retirement to raise this child. She may have forfeited cherished holiday traditions, with some family members no longer attending, though the loss was softened by the joy of welcoming a new child into her life. She gave up "normal" conversations with her family members, who were passed over for raising the child. She has much to grieve and wounds to heal.

But one thing she should not feel is guilt. Her decision was rooted in love, selflessness, and a desire to protect her great-grandchild. While grief is a natural part of this journey, guilt has no rightful place in her heart.

She was a patient who professed Christianity and was familiar with Galatians 5:22-23, where Paul describes the fruit of the Spirit as "love, joy, peace, patience, kindness, goodness, faithfulness, gentleness, and self-control." I gently reminded her that guilt was not on that list and was not from the Holy Spirit but rather from the enemy. I encouraged her to metaphorically drop the guilt she was carrying into the trash on her way out of my office. She left with a smile, visibly lighter. While guilt was not severely controlling her life, it was likely stealing small daily victories and robbing her of the peace she could have otherwise fully embraced. Letting go of that guilt allowed her to take another step toward the freedom and joy God desires for us.

I've met many others who struggle with guilt over something they did in the past. What we must understand is that we don't have the privilege of hindsight at the moment we need to make decisions. We must find peace in knowing that we made the best decision we could at the time, given the information we had. Sometimes we make good decisions, and sometimes we make bad ones, but the key is to learn from them and move forward.

A friend once asked me what my biggest regret was, and I refused to answer. We should not live in our regrets. Yet, over the years, I've had many people argue with me about this. For some, holding on to guilt feels almost like a badge of honor. They believe, somewhere in their mind, that their "bad" is somehow so much more "bad" than everyone else's "bad." But what we often forget is that God's "good" is infinitely greater than our "bad."

I was raised in a secular household and believed that science could explain anything. I had never been to church, but I received an excellent education at a magnet school in inner-city Pittsburgh. Growing up in the seventies, a time when women's reproductive freedom was gaining momentum, I was taught how to prevent pregnancy but not about the value of abstinence. And no one mentioned that baby oil could cause condom failure.

I saw myself as a modern woman in control of her destiny. So, when I became pregnant as a teenager, I had no doubt that I would have an abortion.

I went through with it and moved on with my life. I met another man who would later become my husband. After several years of marriage, we felt a strong desire to have children.

Despite my efforts with menstrual cycle monitoring, reproductive hormones, and infertility treatments, science could not explain my infertility, and the treatments were ineffective. In short, science failed me. I began to wonder if there was more to conception than random chance and basic biology.

The grief cycle of infertility is unique in that there is a new loss every month. This recurring grief can wear you down. I found myself desperately longing for what I had so carelessly thrown away in my teenage years. The guilt that followed was indescribable.

I remember meeting with a pastor at a local church. I tearfully shared about my abortion, and he shrugged and said, "It is forgiven." Did he not understand how "bad" my "bad" was? He used several analogies to help me understand that Jesus paid the penalty for my sins. With each analogy, I countered with how horrible a person I was. After over an hour of discussion, he finally broke through when he said, "I don't want to minimize the guilt that you feel, but since the Holy God of the universe has forgiven you, maybe you can forgive yourself." That's when I accepted Jesus as my Lord and Savior. For years, I have pondered that shrug this pastor gave me when I first confessed my sin, and I imagine Jesus doing the same. Hebrews 8:12 says, "For I will forgive their wickedness and will remember their sins no more." *No more*! And yet, after we are saved, some of us still carry our sins around as a heavy burden, cheapening the gift Jesus gave us when he paid the ultimate penalty for our past, present, and future sins.

God is all-knowing and all-powerful. He knew exactly what I would do in response to my teen pregnancy, and He knew exactly how He would use my abortion to bring me to Himself years later. God wasn't surprised by your sin either. The devil was using intense guilt as a last-ditch effort to retain my soul. Is he trying to do the same to you or someone you love? Once the devil loses our souls, we cannot let him use guilt to make us unfruitful Christians.

God did not send His only Son to take on human form, endure beating, mockery, crucifixion, and even Hell for three days, just to forgive everyone *except* you. If the Holy God of the universe can forgive you, then perhaps it's time to follow His example and forgive yourself.

Pride

Pride is a bit tricky because it shows up in the strangest of places. If you look hard enough, you may have seen it in the earlier section: "My bad is more bad than your bad." Really. Are you truly that special? I don't think so.

Proverbs 16:18 says, "Pride goes before destruction, a haughty spirit before a fall." Pride says I know better than you do. Pride was the source of Adam and Eve's failure in the Garden of Eden, for they believed they could be "like God, knowing good and evil" (Gen 3:4b).

The Bible says that our life is "like a breath" and our "days are like a fleeting shadow" (Psalm 144:4). Following God's will should be the paramount focus of our lives. I don't deserve anything that I have; in fact, I don't deserve my very next breath. Yet God allows it. He has given me my spouse, my children, my house, and my career. He has given me the words for this book. I can do nothing apart from Him. All of the glory should go to Him. I don't deserve to be listened to, nor do I deserve an outlet for my ministry, other than what God wills in the form of fruit He intends me to bear.

God gives us a warning in 1 John 2:16: "For everything in the world—the lust of the flesh, the lust of the eyes, and the pride of life—comes not from the

Father but from the world." Neil Anderson in *The Bondage Breaker* reminds us:

> *Whenever you feel that you don't need God's help or direction, that you can handle your life without consulting Him, that you don't need to bow the knee to anyone, beware: That's the pride of life. You may think you are serving yourself, but whenever you stop worshipping and serving God you are in reality worshipping and serving Satan--which is what he wants more than anything else.*

Serving Satan? Ouch! Pride is the root behind many sins, big and small.

I remember a time when I thought I deserved my kids' obedience. God blessed me with two wonderful children who have good hearts and a passion for God. They have spared me many of the more significant struggles that other parents face. Yet, like all kids, they sometimes get distracted and don't do the things they are supposed to do as promptly as they should. In my younger parenting years, I used to get pretty angry.

I initially believed that I was simply hardwired to be angry and couldn't do anything about it. I was born to an explosive parent, so perhaps this is just my destiny. Yet this was a deception from the enemy! I kept finding myself back in a state of anger when my kids would not complete their tasks promptly. Eventually, God showed me that my problem was pride. I will cover this story in more detail in Chapter 11 but offer some preliminary comments here.

I am supposed to discipline my children (Proverbs 13:24), providing Godly instruction, so they grow fruitful in Christ. Children are called in Scripture to obey their parents (Ephesians 6:1). I am supposed to discipline them, and they are supposed to obey me, but do I *deserve* their obedience? If I answer yes, I may be doomed to anger, which is not a fruit of the Spirit. If I answer no, I am more likely to keep a cool head and provide more effective, Godly discipline as God leads me at that moment. One choice is of the flesh, and the other is of the Spirit. My kids *should* obey me, but not because I *deserve* it.

When we address the hooks of unforgiveness, guilt, and pride, we begin to experience the fullness of the freedom Christ has already won for us. We are no longer trapped in sin's cycle but empowered to walk in victory.

When we are saved, we are made a new creation, so why is this "old flesh" still hanging around? What choice must we make to live out the truth of our new self? This requires us to come to terms with our "old" man.

CHAPTER 8

GETTING A HANDLE ON THE OLD MAN

Second Corinthians 5:17 says that in Christ we are a new creation. "The old has gone, the new is here!" With this new man comes the indwelling Holy Spirit, who fills us with love, joy, peace, patience, kindness, goodness, faithfulness, gentleness, and self-control (Galatians 5:22-23). Yet I've had many days where the old man seems to return, causing confusion. Before salvation, we were sinners saved by grace. Now we are seated with Christ in the heavenly realms (Ephesians 2:6) and have a full abundance of his life living in us. We are now "fellow citizens with the saints and members of the household of God" (Ephesians 2:19), made perfect with the life of Christ. Yet though we are saints, we also sin from time to time. How do we reconcile this paradox?

Bill Gilliam, in his book *Lifetime Guarantee*, does an excellent job explaining the tripartite nature of our being: body, soul, and spirit. When we are saved, the spirit is made alive with Christ in a process often called justification. Our soul is made up of our mind, emotions, and will, and it is undergoing the process of sanctification. Our body, the earth suit we currently inhabit, will later be glorified. Yet right now, it continues to be the same earth suit that we had before we were saved. This earth suit contains a brain with firmly established neural networks consistent with our old patterns of behavior. When we get saved, there is no reset button to wipe out all that old programming.

Imagine receiving a used smartphone from a friend. One of the first things you'd likely do is reset it to factory defaults. This removes the old data, apps, and settings, allowing you to start fresh. But, unlike a smartphone, there's no way to reset our brains to factory settings. And honestly, we wouldn't want that anyway. Our lives before Christ are full of meaningful memories—relationships, joys, and experiences that shaped us. God uses these relationships to witness to others, even though those same old patterns can sometimes resurface and challenge us.

When we read the story of creation in Genesis, we learned that Adam was able to converse with God, eat solid food, walk in the garden, and perform his tasks as assigned by God. Adam was born as a man, with adult abilities to reason and make decisions, in direct and immediate communion with his father. In contrast, every human since Adam and Eve has been born as a baby. We spend our earliest years separated spiritually from God, trying to figure out how to get our needs met independently of Christ. Bill Gilliam says we learn to be "lord of our ring." As babies, we cry when hungry or need a diaper change. As we grow, we develop patterns—some positive, some harmful—that help us navigate life. We are also raised in a fallen world, full of imperfect people who sometimes disappoint us. Broken promises, profound loss, and other painful experiences create strong neural pathways in our brains, what Gilliam refers to as "green superhighways." The enemy exploits these superhighways to attack us, often triggering strong emotions and misguided thoughts. The devil knows how to push our buttons, even though sometimes we ourselves don't know what those buttons are.

I once had a patient share some difficult things going on in her life, which made her quite tearful in my office. It became obvious that she was coping fairly well and had strong faith to help her overcome the challenges of her situation. In her humanity, the struggles led to tears of grief. Yet when it was time to leave, she knew it was time to pull herself together and get back to her life. As she was walking out, she said, "It's time to change the channel." In essence, that is exactly what we have to do!

Bill Gilliam talks about spiritual warfare from the perspective of tuning in to two different "channels." A modified version of his "first channel" is depicted in the diagram below, and the hash marks in the brain represent the "green superhighways." Note that before you were saved, you had a "dead" spirit, and the flesh channel was your only input source.

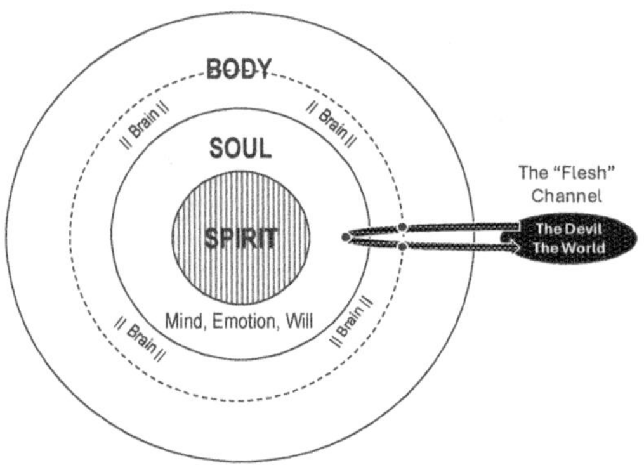

External forces interface with your body through your five senses, and your brain processes those inputs and delivers them to your mind and emotions. Your will then utilizes your body to interface back with the world.

The devil, utilizing the power of sin that exists within our body, takes advantage of these "green superhighways" in our old memory banks to initiate strong emotions and false thoughts that are counterproductive to our Christian walk. He cannot have our soul, yet he will do whatever he can to prevent us from bearing fruit for Christ. I like to call this the "flesh channel."

Once we are saved, we become a new creation in Christ. Jesus + Me = The New Me.

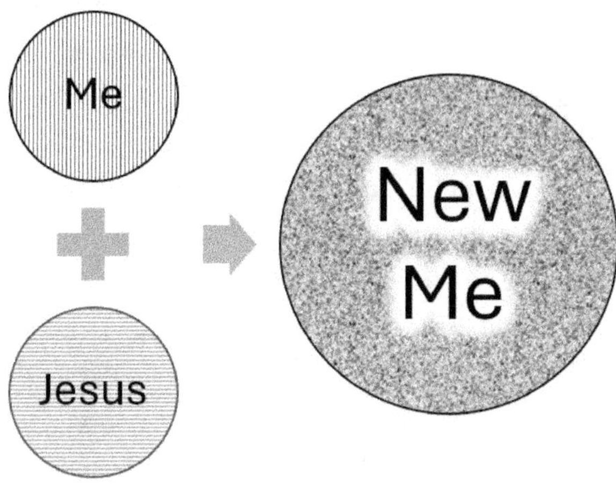

And hence, our spirit becomes a new spirit:

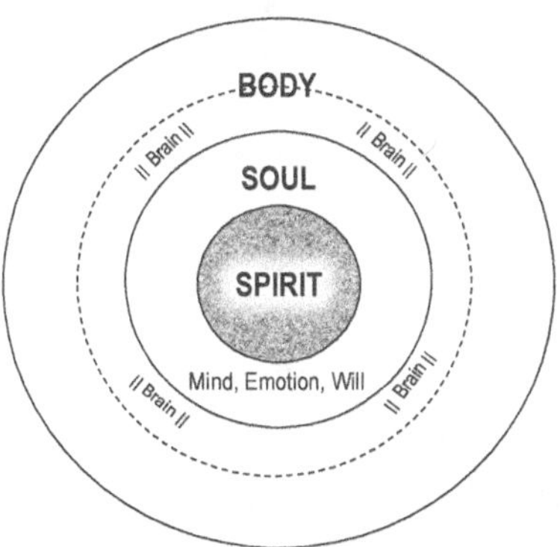

Because this is true, we now have another choice, which is to fix our minds on things above. The Bible tells us that we are to "take captive every thought to make it obedient to Christ" (2 Corinthians 10:5). It should be a regular habit for us to spend time alone with God daily, tuning in to His will in our lives. We are to focus on the wise counsel found in Philippians 4:8: "Whatever is good, whatever is noble, whatever is right, whatever is pure, whatever is lovely, whatever is admirable--if anything is excellent or praiseworthy--think about such things." We are to focus our minds on the positive. As we practice this regularly, we will find our minds turning more and more often to what I will call the "spirit channel."

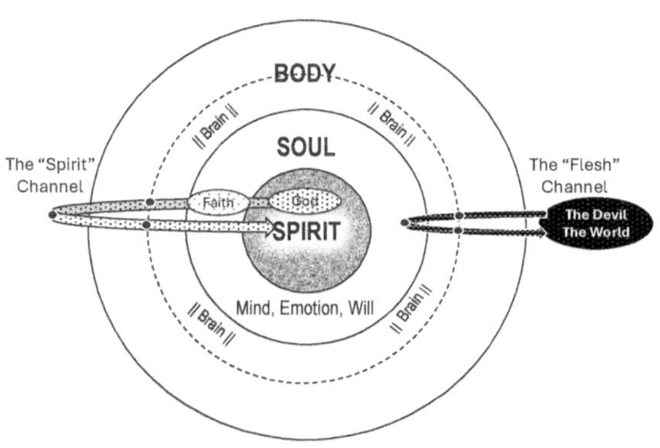

The spirit channel uses the indwelling Holy Spirit as the source. Being focused inward, our spirit uses our mind, emotions, and will through faith to interface with our body, which will interact with the world to bear fruit for God. As we stay tuned into the spirit channel, we will begin to place roadblocks to the flesh channel to defend against the green superhighways that filter into our minds. We can learn to take every thought captive to the obedience of Christ. The combined channels and the "roadblock" look like this:

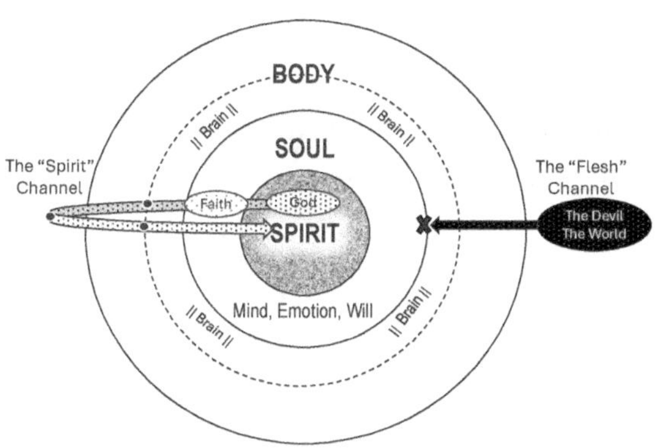

Bill Gilliam makes it clear that handling emotions is a bit more complicated. In many cases, our emotional responses to past experiences are strong and difficult. I believe they are sometimes generated from out-of-balance brain biochemistry that simply needs medication to control. Yet while these emotions are often inconvenient, they are also the source of joy and love, which are so important to the expression of our Christian faith. God wants to use our emotions to refine us. As we choose the path of obedience despite our emotions, we become more mature in Christ. God smiles, and the enemy shrieks.

God makes us all different. Some are "doers," others are "feelers," and most are a combination of both. God needs to use all types of people. If your house floods, you will want to call in your "doer" friend, who will suck the water out of your carpet and help you repair damaged drywall. Yet if you lose precious treasures in the flood which makes you sad, you may also want to call in your "feeler" friend, who will sit next to you knee-to-knee and console you. God needs all types of people. Our emotions are not wrong and often reflect a beautiful expression of our humanity. Yet sometimes our emotions cannot be trusted.

Bill Gilliam describes this with an analogy of a person being chased by a bear. The person quickly enters into a sturdy cabin in the woods, slams the door shut, and immediately becomes safe. While the camper may not initially know that the cabin is sturdy, the truth is that he is safe whether he believes it or not. He may still be emotionally upset and screaming, glued to the wall at the other end of the cabin, yet the fact that he feels unsafe does not change the fact that he is safe.

Step One. TRUTH—I *am* safe.

After a short time, the camper may begin to realize that the bear cannot penetrate the door or the walls. The one remaining window is much too small for the bear to enter. He may even begin to notice that the walls are constructed of thick oak logs stacked and secured with metal struts. While his body might still be glued to the cabin wall, he now begins to understand in his mind that he is, in fact, safe.

Step Two. FAITH—I *know* I am safe.

Once he is convinced he is safe, the camper will begin to realize that there is other square footage of the cabin which is also safe, and his pulse rate and respiratory rate are not healthy for him. He will begin to step away from the cabin wall, into the center of the cabin. He will begin investigating his surroundings and checking his mobile phone for a cellular signal. He will start to make a plan. In short, he will begin to act like a person who is safe.

Step Three. WORKS—I begin to *act* safe.

At this point in Bill Gilliam's book, he reflects his sense of humor:

Step Four. FEELINGS—I begin to *feel* safe, *sort of*.

The reality is it will take a while before the camper's emotions settle down in a situation like this. He can do some deep breathing techniques, yet it will take time for his pulse and breathing rate to return to normal. He may pull out his cell phone and call for help with trembling fingers. The fear of that event may linger well throughout the day, and into his dreams for many nights. There is no fast "reset switch" for an emotional event like that. *Feeling safe is a process.*

Sometimes we cannot trust our emotions, and we must work within our mind to set our thoughts on truth. If we win the battle for our minds, our emotions will eventually settle in. Put simply, we must have a healthy dose of faith.

CHAPTER 9

REMEMBERING WHO YOU REALLY ARE, AND WHO GOD REALLY IS

I once had a friend who had been smoking since his early teen years. He had tried quitting several times, only to relapse—just like many smokers do. But one day, as he watched his young children pretend to smoke their macaroni and cheese at the dinner table, something clicked. That day, he became a non-smoker.

Many people say that smokers can quit once they "make up their mind" to do so, but it's not that simple. My friend still struggled for a while with the classic physical and emotional withdrawal symptoms. He took medication to help curb the cravings, and it worked well, but this wasn't the secret to his success. The real breakthrough came when he changed his perspective about who he was. He stopped seeing himself as a *smoker trying to quit.* Instead, he saw himself as *a non-smoker who craved a cigarette.* That shift in identity made all the difference.

He wanted a cigarette, but this was no longer consistent with who he was. He saw himself as a non-smoker, and that changed everything.

Who You Really Are:

This brings us to a key principle. When you are unsaved, you are a sinner who needs to be saved by grace. During the process of salvation, you are a sinner getting saved by grace. But after you're saved, you become a saint.

Now, I know what you're thinking. You don't always feel like a saint. You didn't suddenly start acting perfectly once you were saved, and you still sometimes struggle with sin. But the Bible is clear: in 1 Corinthians 1:2, it calls you a saint. Sin is no longer consistent with your true identity. Yes, we still sin—this is the struggle of Christian life. You're not alone in this.

The Christian walk is challenging, but it becomes much more fruitful when we see ourselves as God sees us—as saints. When we believe we have power over sin, we are more likely to overcome it. The devil wants us to believe we are helpless sinners who cannot control our behavior. This mindset makes us vulnerable to temptation, and that's exactly what the enemy wants.

The truth is, you are a saint.

The Only Math Problem in Sunday School Class

Now, let's talk about a math equation and infinity.

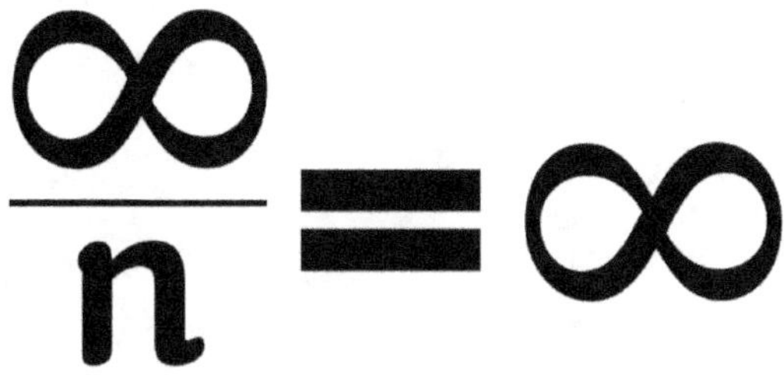

In algebra, if you multiply anything by infinity, you get infinity. And if you divide infinity by any number, you still get infinity. So, when God gives you a piece of the Holy Spirit to dwell within you, how much of it do you get? An infinite amount of all of God's good things: love, peace, joy, and acceptance!

God also has complete authority over the devil. When Jesus died on the cross and defeated sin and death, He utterly conquered Satan in his own domain. Jesus has complete authority over the devil, and when you got saved, a piece of Jesus came to live inside of you. So, if Jesus has authority over the devil, and He lives in you, how much authority do you have? *You have the same authority as Jesus Himself!*

When you were saved, you became a saint, indwelt by the Holy Spirit. You are no longer a helpless victim of sin, and you have all the authority you need to send the devil back to the slimy hole he crawled out of. But if you don't believe this, then the devil will exploit this unbelief and make you think you're still a helpless sinner who can't stop sinning. How you see yourself matters! You are no longer a helpless sinner saved by grace; you are now a saint!

Who God Really Is

Many Christians think they are stuck in a cosmic tug of war, with God and all good things pulling them in one direction, and the devil and sin pulling them in the other.

However, this couldn't be further from the truth. God is not some external force pulling you in a good direction—He lives within you and wants to work in your mind and emotions, empowering you to will the right actions. You and God are inextricably linked. The old you is dead. You have God's infinite power living inside of you, and infinity divided by any number is still infinity! You have more than enough power to overcome the battle with sin. With the knowledge of truth within you, you can hold up a stop sign to the devil's influences, shutting down his entry into your mind.

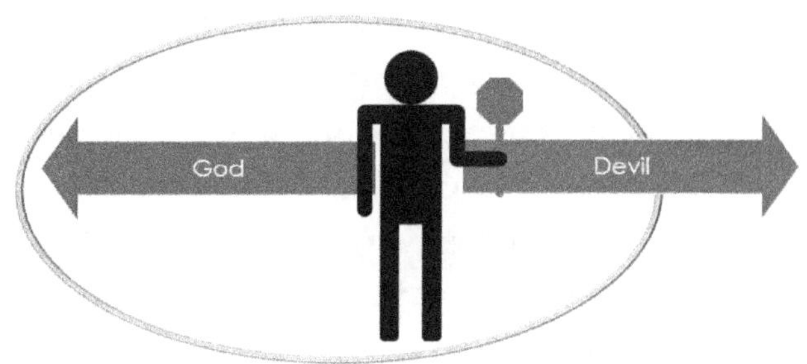

In fact, when we try to compare God's power with the devil's power, there's really no comparison. I am limited by the size of this page and the font available for this text, yet if we were to try to depict God's power compared to the devil's power, it may look something like this:

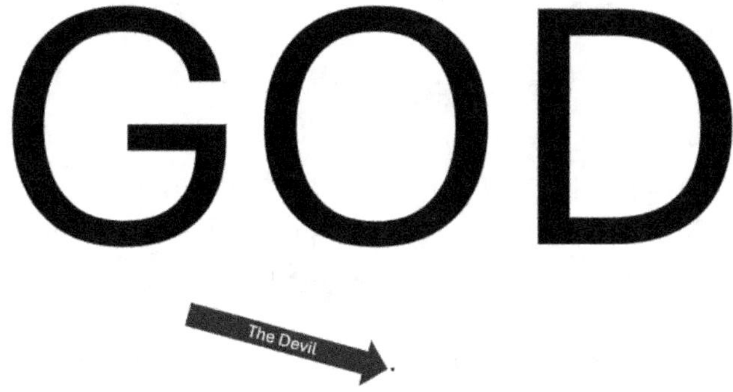

The devil is a dot! When God defeated sin and death by raising Jesus from the grave on the third day, the devil was reduced to nothing—like a bug squashed into the carpet. His power compared to God's is minuscule. And you have the same authority over the devil that Jesus had when He walked the earth!

The singer-songwriter Jeremy Camp co-wrote a song with Jason Ingram called *Same Power*, which drives this point home. The same power that raised Jesus, commanded the dead to wake, moved mountains, and calmed raging seas lives in us. If you need to be reminded about the power of Christ in you, I recommend you listen to this song on repeat.

So, if we have the same power and authority over the devil that Jesus had, why do we still sin? The simple answer is that we don't fully understand the authority we've been given, nor recognize that the authority is ours to wield.

The Magic of the Fruit of the Spirit

Galatians 5:22-23 tells us that the fruit of the Spirit is love, joy, peace, patience, kindness, goodness, faithfulness, gentleness, and self-control. How much of the Spirit's power do you receive when the Holy Spirit indwells you? An *infinite* amount. So, how many of these fruits can you bear? An *infinite* amount.

Consider how this applies to marital conflicts. Both spouses may have their share of unforgiveness, pride, guilt, and sadness. They each carry old memories and thought patterns that make them feel stuck. If both are saved, then both have an infinite amount of love available to them from the indwelling Holy Spirit. If they could choose to extend grace and let love prevail, their marriage would grow stronger.

The challenge is to let it flow and reject the old feelings. It is easier said than done, yet completely possible.

1 Corinthians 13:4-8 tells us:

Love is patient. Love is kind. It does not envy, it does not boast, it is not proud. It does not dishonor others, it is not self-seeking, it is not easily angered, it keeps no record of wrongs. Love does not delight in evil but rejoices with the truth. It always protects, always trusts, always hopes, always perseveres.

You have an infinite amount of this kind of love living inside of you, whether you believe it or not. And you have this infinite amount of love for your spouse, your family, and your friends.

I close with a story to illustrate my point. My parents divorced when I was about two years old, leaving my mom to raise my brother and me as a single parent. From a young age, I knew I wanted a career to avoid the financial struggles my mother faced. I dedicated myself to my studies, determined to succeed.

My relationship with my biological father was never strong, though I respected him during his visits. When I proudly showed him my first report card with straight A's, he dismissed my achievement because I would "just get married and have kids anyway." While there's nothing wrong with being a homemaker, I knew that wasn't my path. I resented my father's response and walked out on him, seeking solace at a friend's house.

Years later, a friend blocked me from pursuing something that I felt I had the skills to do. In hindsight, I realize my timing was poor and my friend's decision was proper, yet my frustration over this sent me into a tailspin. The anger allowed the enemy to gain a foothold in my life, leading to one of the fiercest personal spiritual warfare struggles I've ever faced. I shudder to think of the damage I could have caused without my spiritual warfare training. I was tempted by the enemy to make my frustration public to his family and friends, go over his head, and even considered leaving my church, abandoning the rich relationships I had there. I couldn't sleep and cried often. The enemy tried to turn me against my husband because he sided with my friend. Again, in hindsight, their decision was proper, but I struggled to manage my raw emotions at the time.

Finally, the Holy Spirit broke through. I was exhausted from being upset and angry, but more than that, I missed the rich relationship I had with my friend's wife. I had to forgive and move on. The only force strong enough to overcome such negative emotions is love. You have an infinite amount of love within you, so grab onto it and embrace it! As I emerged from this dark place, the Holy Spirit inspired me to write this essay.

I Want My Friend Back

Have you ever had your feelings hurt by a close friend?

I don't consider myself a hyper-emotional person, yet we all have our weaknesses. Sometimes it is a hurtful childhood experience that makes us hypersensitive to one certain thing in our lives. I promise you, the devil knows that one certain thing. A lot of the time, though, your friends do not.

My friend stepped all over that one certain thing recently. He didn't mean to, yet once it happened, there was no turning back. He disagreed with me on that one certain thing, as it is his right to do. He didn't mean to upset me, yet he found himself balancing precariously over a huge expanse of emotional quicksand. Tread lightly, or you might sink fast.

Lucky for me, he is a composed, mature Christian who can hold himself together. I kept trying to turn away from this hurt, yet the devil knew just where to find me. He wanted me to turn away from my friend and my church. He wanted me to breed dissension. He wanted me to give up 20 years of relationships from long-term attendance at the same church. He wanted me to be emotional in the sanctuary and lose credibility with my peers. He saw this one certain thing as his gateway to minimize my witness. He was relentless.

During those weeks, I had ups and downs, with days when I was doing pretty well and days when I was not. The hardest days were church days, where that *<u>one certain thing</u>* *ended up being visible to me in many different ways. The devil knew how to call my attention to that* *<u>one certain thing</u>* *that had in the past been innocuously present around me. My church, usually a place where I hear God and have peace, was instead a battleground of much distress. I used many spiritual warfare tactics to hold myself together and prevent harsh words, yet some days my shield of faith was weak. I think some Christians, when faced with a similar assault, might have simply walked away from it all. The temptation to do so was real.*

I was so tired of being distressed, yet I wasn't sure how to move past it. I knew my friend didn't mean to hurt me, and I thought I had forgiven him, yet I was still just really sad. I could not see a path towards peace when the enemy kept tossing that *<u>one certain thing</u>* *back in my face. I wasn't sure how to turn away from it.*

I finally realized that I wanted my friend back. And I wanted his wife back, for God had steered me away from her also to avoid sowing dissent in their marriage. In truth, my friends never left me, I was the one distancing myself. Yet love always wins over sadness, anger, and pride. I was tired, and I had come to the end of myself. I had found something stronger than *<u>that one certain thing</u>*. *My love for my friends was greater.*

IV

Putting it All Together

CHAPTER 10

THE POWER OF THE SHIELD OF FAITH

Faith can be a fickle thing. Hebrews 11:1 tells us that "faith is being sure of what we hope for and certain of what we do not see." We can possess great gifts—truth, righteousness, salvation, and peace. Yet, if we don't believe we truly have these gifts, what good are they to us?

Imagine receiving a call from an attorney across the country telling you that a long-lost uncle has passed away and left you a million dollars. You might dismiss the call as a prank, thinking nothing of it. But if this were true, and you continued to live your life as if it were not true, what would you lose? You'd lose a million dollars!

Similarly, if we have truth, love, and all the fruit of the Spirit but don't believe we possess them, we lose their impact on our lives. This is why the devil relentlessly attacks our faith. Faith is essential in winning the battle for our minds.

When we look at the armor of God as Paul describes in Ephesians 6:13-17, we are told to stand firm with the belt of truth, the breastplate of righteousness, and our feet fitted with the readiness that comes from the gospel of peace. But then we are instructed to take up the helmet of salvation, the shield of faith, and the sword of the Spirit, which is the Word of God. What does it mean to take up these pieces of armor? How do we wield them?

In Chapter 7, we explored how the devil exploits emotions like guilt, pride, and unforgiveness—rooted in unbelief. Do we truly believe that God can do what He says He will do? Do we believe He has sent His Son to live in us, exerting His authority through us? Do we believe we are saints? Do we believe we have authority over the devil?

If we believe these things, it becomes easier to shed the hooks of bondage that the enemy uses to hold us captive. We may stumble in our humanity, but forgiveness is always available, and we must never resign ourselves to thinking there's no way out of our struggles.

Imagine a scenario where a wife has a green super-highway for self-sufficiency, which is a form of pride. Prior to becoming saved and knowing she had a loving God who wanted to lead her, she spent years seeking education and building her career to forge her own path in this world. If her desired path is not what God intends in His timing, doors may shut to her plan. Others around her, such as her husband, may be the instrument that God uses to disrupt her plans.

Imagine what the devil can do with that! How might he exploit a woman with a green superhighway of self-sufficiency if her husband took action to shut a door to her plans? The devil will deliver "betrayal" straight to her green superhighway to generate explosive emotions in her feeler. What might this do to her passion for ministry? What might this do to her marriage? How might a woman dig her way out of this cesspool of negative emotions?

Let's review Bill Gillham's four steps to handling your emotions, discussed previously in Chapter 8:

Step One. TRUTH—I am <u>safe.</u>

Step Two. FAITH—I know I am <u>safe.</u>

Step Three. WORKS—I begin to act <u>safe.</u>

Step Four. FEELINGS—I begin to feel <u>safe</u>, *sort of.*

However, I believe there is a vital step before Step One: We need to know what goes in that blank! I am <u>secure</u>. I am <u>loved</u>. I am <u>accepted</u>. I am a <u>saint</u>. I am <u>God's child</u>. I am <u>useful</u>.

Albert Einstein is credited as having said, "If I had an hour to solve a problem, I'd spend 55 minutes thinking about the problem and 5 minutes thinking about the solution." In the same way, we must first identify our grievances and the wounds that lie beneath them before we can move toward healing.

For example, this woman might feel unloved, even though her husband truly loves her. She might feel betrayed, even though he's simply trying to lead her in the best way he knows. She may be discouraged by the closed doors in her life, unaware that God might be leading her down a different path. The war will be fought in her mind as she comes to understand the truth about her husband's actions and God's plan.

Yet, this process takes time. She needs to feel secure, loved, and accepted again. Her husband should lovingly support her during this period of emotional turmoil. But often, the situation escalates because the husband, too, feels disrespected. He might yell back when she yells and criticize when she criticizes. He may be triggered by deep-seated insecurities, perhaps linked to past rejections. In his mind, his wife's behavior signals disrespect, when in reality, she's simply struggling to process her emotions. Rather than showing compassion, he retreats in frustration. And the devil couldn't be happier.

There is a better way, and it involves wielding our shield of faith.

CHAPTER 11

GETTING OFF THE HAMSTER WHEEL OF TORMENT

We've explored the devil's tactics—deception, temptation, and condemnation—as well as the emotions he exploits: unforgiveness, guilt, and pride. But how does it all fit together?

The "**Sin → Confess → Repent**" cycle can be exhausting. We sin, acknowledge our sin, feel remorse, and then the cycle repeats with the next assault. We've learned that in Christ, we are new creations, and sin is no longer our nature. Yet, it still happens. We must recognize that often, when we sin, we are being triggered by the enemy.

If we blame ourselves, we feel hopeless. If we blame God, our confidence in Him is shattered. But if we place the blame on the devil, we can align our thoughts properly. This doesn't mean we can say, "The devil made me do it." We each have a responsibility to stand firm against the enemy and take every thought captive for Christ. However, understanding the devil's tactics can help us break free.

When we're stuck, the cycle often looks like this:

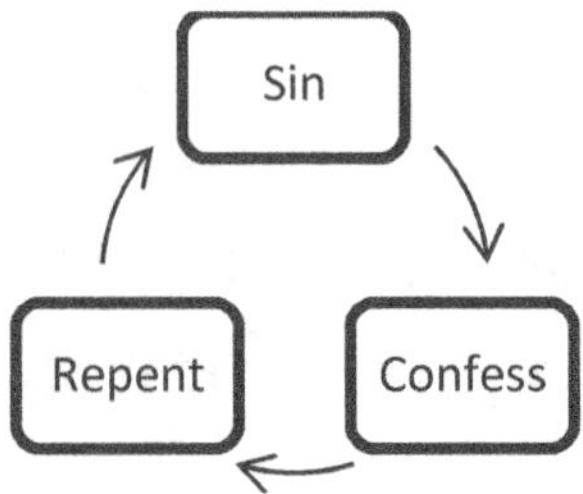

Imagine tying soap to a string. If you swing the rope around, the soap cannot break free because you're holding the rope. The question is: *What hook is holding your rope?*

As we've seen, the root of many struggles is unbelief, which can manifest as guilt, pride, or unforgiveness. The "flaming arrows of the evil one" (Ephesians 6:16)—deception, temptation, and condemnation—usually trigger this cycle. To break free, we must use the shield of faith—not just to know the truth but to believe it. Adding spiritual warfare to the diagram looks like this:

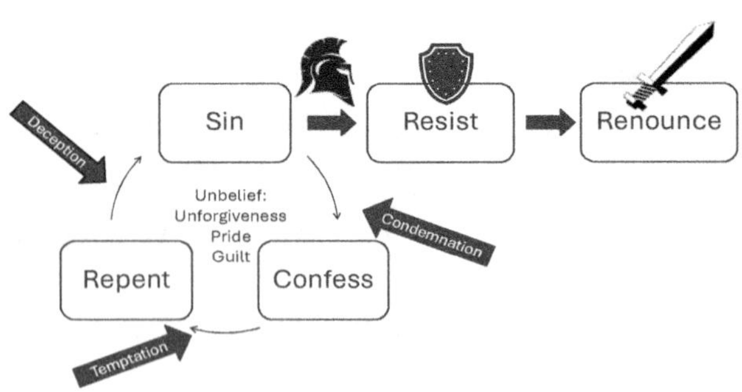

The helmet protects our head. While Ephesians 6:17 calls this the helmet of salvation, I like to imagine it also protecting my thoughts as I accept salvation freely offered to me. We **resist** with our shield as we harness faith to accept the truth. We **renounce** with the sword of the spirit, which is the Word of God. We say scripture out loud. We pray. As Jesus did when he was tempted by Satan in the desert, we should use scripture as our weapon to counteract lies. With that same mouth, we renounce the sin and declare our departure from it.

There is much value in outwardly rebuking the devil. One of my favorite Christian movie scenes is from *The War Room,* where the character named Elizabeth Jordan sends the devil out of her house. But in the process of rebuking the devil, she also effectively renounced her old way of thinking, working, and communicating with her spouse. The transformation within her home because of this decision was striking, leading to better marital harmony and her spouse's renewed faith. Her mentor's happy dance later in the film is one of my other favorite Christian movie clips.

Usually, there is some form of unforgiveness, pride, or guilt that the devil uses as his "foothold," and he leverages the tactics of deception, temptation, and condemnation to restart the cycle. It starts because we believe a lie, but often we can't identify it. The devil doesn't want you to know what it is or realize his involvement.

Note that once you are saved, your future is secure. Some Christians live bitter, unrepentant lives but are still saved. Neither repentance nor renouncing sin is required to maintain that salvation. But renouncing sets you free from the devil's lies. Renouncing says that I have walked away from that sin, and I am not going back. It is crossing a line and declaring that the old you is not who you are anymore. That success occurs only once you truly *believe* the truth.

I struggled with a particular "crazy cycle" for years myself before I could identify my own personal hook.

I used to become quite angry while disciplining my children. We are blessed with two wonderful kids, who, at heart, want to do the right thing. But like all kids, they sometimes aren't perfect. They may get distracted when asked to do something, or they may need reminders, especially when it's getting late, and they need to go to bed for school the next day. And sometimes, after multiple reminders, "Drill Sergeant Mom" would make an appearance.

I would bang on their doors, yell at the top of my lungs, and bark commands like:

- Put your clothes on!
- Brush your teeth!

- Pick up your clothes!
- Get in bed!

The goal was to get them to bed efficiently so they could be well-rested for the next day. But did my tirade contribute to a peaceful, restful bedtime? Absolutely not! Instead, we all became tense and upset. My daughter might cry, and the anger would escalate. Rather than helping them get to bed faster, my out-of-control actions caused even more chaos. We'd all be up for another hour, angry and frustrated.

When I calmed down, the Holy Spirit would gently prompt me to apologize, which I would do. I'd confess and repent. But then, not too long later, the cycle would repeat. Why? Because I didn't understand the root of the problem. I believed my anger was simply part of my Type A personality and that there was nothing I could do about it. It felt hopeless and exhausting.

While teaching a Bible study on *The Bondage Breaker* by Neil Anderson, God revealed to me the cause of my struggle: **pride**.

I had developed a prideful belief that I *deserved* my kids' obedience. After all, the Bible commands children to obey their parents, and I felt that I had a God-given responsibility to discipline them. But disciplining them isn't just about enforcing obedience;

it's about leading them toward the most desirable outcome.

I wanted them to get to bed quickly, yet my "Drill Sergeant Mom" approach was counterproductive. Galatians 5:22-23 teaches that the fruit of the Spirit includes love, joy, peace, patience, kindness, goodness, faithfulness, gentleness, and self-control. Were any of those qualities present in my "Drill Sergeant Mom" persona? Absolutely not! There was no love, kindness, peace, or joy in my actions, and I certainly wasn't showing self-control. I wasn't reflecting the Holy Spirit.

The wiser approach would have been to calmly assess the situation and remove the distractions causing the problem. If I had done that, the outcome would have been much better. Another strategy would have been to wait and discuss the issue the next night at dinner, involving my children in brainstorming ways to make the bedtime routine more efficient. This kind of parenting is true discipleship, not the frantic barking of orders.

I realized that pride was the hook in the "sin → confess → repent cycle." I felt entitled to my children's obedience. But God reminded me that I deserve nothing! I don't even deserve my next breath, let alone the children I've been entrusted with. They are a gift from God, and my role is to parent and protect them—not because I "deserve" it, but because it's what's best for them. If they learn to obey me, they may also be better equipped to obey God, which is far more important.

Pride was my downfall. The cure was to eliminate pride, but I also had to believe—I had to have faith—that I possess all the love, joy, peace, and patience I need to be a better parent. As of the time of writing, "Drill Sergeant Mom" has been gone for over eight years, never to return. Sure, I still feel the urge to get angry sometimes, but when that happens, I remind myself of my true identity in Christ.

Luke 22:31-34 records a foreshadowing of Peter's pending spiritual failure:

> *"Simon, Simon, Satan has asked to sift all of you as wheat. But I have prayed for you, Simon, that your faith may not fail. And when you have turned back, strengthen your brothers."*
>
> *But he replied, "Lord, I am ready to go with you to prison and to death."*
>
> *Jesus answered, "I tell you, Peter, before the rooster crows today, you will deny three times that you know me."*

Peter's pride blinded him, leaving him vulnerable to the devil's deception.

Acts 5 recounts the story of Ananias and Sapphira, who sold property to use for the ministry but kept back a part of the money for themselves. Their great sin was that they lied about it. Their pride led them to believe they could get away with it, but their deception, fueled by the devil's temptation for recognition and money, resulted in their deaths. Thankfully, God's punishment is not usually as severe today.

Tax collectors in Jesus' time were despised, and Matthew, the son of Alphaeus, was one of them (Mark 2:14). It's difficult to imagine the depth of guilt Matthew must have felt or the condemnation he faced from the devil. But it was Matthew's faith in Jesus that broke him free from that lifestyle and transformed him into a disciple.

We cannot wield the shield of faith if we have the truth but don't believe it. But as we learn to lean into the truth, new patterns of behavior emerge.

We must recognize the "hooks" of unforgiveness, pride, and guilt in our lives and trust God, through faith, to remove them. When we do, we disarm the enemy. When we do, we break free.

CHAPTER 12

THE PROBLEM WITH ANGER

Scripture speaks of anger, and God certainly expresses righteous anger. However, for us, 'righteous' anger is often just a mask for our own wounded pride. Because our hearts are not purely holy like God's, our anger rarely stays righteous for long.

Returning to the Christian walk analogy from Chapter 5, remember we are not called to yell at the windows. The battle over sin and death has already been won, so it is our job to keep our eyes on Jesus and keep walking down the middle of the road. While the indwelling Holy Spirit calls us to stand firm against unrighteousness, we are not called to do so with fleshly anger. The fruit of the Spirit is love, joy, peace, patience, kindness, goodness, faithfulness, gentleness, and self-control (Galatians 5:22-23). Anger is not on that list.

We all experience anger. When we feel wronged, disrespected, or treated unfairly, it is a natural human response. However, this is not a godly response. And since the source of anger is not the Holy Spirit, you likely have influence from external forces causing you to feel this way.

Let me clarify that in no way do I suggest that anyone should be forced to remain in a toxic relationship. Nor do I suggest that we should fail to stand up for truth or take action to protect our loved ones or the vulnerable. We are simply called to do it in a controlled manner, with a spirit of love and compassion within our hearts.

I've heard many people reference how Jesus "turned the tables over in the temple" (Matthew 21:12-13, Mark 11:15-18) to justify their anger. It is hard to compare a direct attack against God to anything we experience as humans. While Jesus did turn away from those whose hearts were closed and called the Pharisees a "brood of vipers" (Matthew 12:34), he did not seek personal vengeance against them. There are numerous examples of Jesus addressing his foes with love and respect, most notably while hanging on the cross, where he said, "Father, forgive them, for they do not know what they are doing" (Luke 23:34). This is a far cry from seeking personal justice.

Jesus repeatedly emphasizes our need to forgive. As we covered in Chapter 7, bitterness is a poison we drink, hoping to hurt someone else. The father of an Amish girl who was killed in the schoolhouse shooting in Pennsylvania on October 2, 2006, went to the shooter's home on the day of the attack with two Amish elders to offer their condolences and forgiveness to the wife. This was beautifully depicted in the movie *Amish Grace.* The wife addressed the father, acknowledging how difficult it must be for him to have lost his daughter earlier that day. He responded, "It is a deep wound." Do you see what he did? He identified his hurt as a wound, acknowledging that wounds eventually heal. And the main bandage for these kinds of wounds is forgiveness. That visit to her house was as much for his own healing as it was for hers.

Consider the deception that many experience. If I were having trouble paying my bills because a bad actor set up a fraudulent website and stole $1,000 of my money, you would probably have empathy for me. But if you knew I squandered $1,000 on frivolous things, you probably would have less. In the first scenario, I was deceived, which engendered compassion. In the second, I willfully spent it. We must recognize that many people who are doing upsetting things are deceived, and that should engender compassion. They may still face negative consequences in response to their actions, and sometimes this means that the relationship must end to protect ourselves or others. Yet in our hearts, we should not be bitter.

When my kids were younger, there was a child on the bus causing trouble for the bus driver. It was natural for my children to come home angry about the child's actions. However, who taught the child to be disrespectful, and what type of home life does he have? The natural response of my kids was to alienate this boy, yet what would happen if we showed him friendship? That shift is much easier when we approach him with compassion rather than anger. That is exactly what the Amish father did, and he was better for it.

Most people are not drawn to the gospel by people pointing out their faults. They are drawn because of the grace given by Jesus to forgive their faults. And that same Spirit lives in us. We don't just *have* forgiveness, we *are* forgiveness. Forgiveness lives in us, and it is our duty to express it.

I grew up with a very bitter great-grandmother, and I never knew her any other way. She liked few people. Thankfully, she liked me, but my friends were not good enough. Most of my mother's boyfriends were not good enough. We lived in Pittsburgh at the time, with narrow two and three-story houses stacked next to each other like sardines. She didn't like the neighbors and talked to very few of them. She would watch them through the windows, then be critical of the things she saw.

She lived in the home with her daughter and son-in-law, and they weren't good enough either. The toilet paper was too thin. My grandfather's cigars stunk. She would be happy when her son came to visit.

Her husband died before I was born. I saw old pictures of him in a wheelchair and learned he had multiple sclerosis, a neurological disorder that makes body parts not work right. It often leads to disability and early death. He died of pneumonia in his early 40s.

My great-grandmother cleaned houses for income. It is hard for me to imagine her as an unskilled worker with two children watching her husband die of a disabling disease before the advent of Social Security and Medicare. I was told she was a happy person in her younger years. Hebrews cautions us to ensure "no bitter root grows up to cause trouble and defile many" (Hebrews 12:15b). While I'm not totally sure what changed her, I suspect his illness and death were the source of her "bitter root."

She didn't like the way one neighbor parked. She did not agree with another neighbor's dating life. Many homes did not have air conditioning, so windows were often left open in the summer to help with air circulation. She would listen to the neighbors argue, then be critical of what she heard. I believe the root of her criticism was this "righteous anger" against people who are not perfect. She would yell at kids walking down the street for various reasons. It wasn't until my adult years that I learned to pity her. The devil's bitter root grew deep into her soul and robbed her of years of joy.

In Chapter 7, I told my abortion story. I understand the fear and worry that young women experience when faced with an unplanned pregnancy. I also recognize that abortion is a polarizing topic, upon which our nation will never agree.

I have spent my entire clinical career involved in the leadership of medical societies. The one I spent the most time with historically had no policy on abortion. The unwritten rule was, if you are trained to do a procedure and it is legal in your state, then they supported you doing it. In my opinion, that was a reasonable compromise. But in 2019, there were nine pro-abortion resolutions brought to the national meeting for the purpose of flipping us from our neutral position to a supportive one. At that time, I felt a clear call to stand up and tell my story.

In general, public speaking is not hard for me. Some people jump out of airplanes to get an adrenaline rush. But for me, put me in front of a big room of people with a microphone and I am happy. However, these two minutes of testimony were the most terrifying of my leadership career. Despite pretreating with a medicine to slow my heart rate, my heart was still pounding. Knowing that this large organization was not going to agree on this topic, my goal was to encourage our organization to stay neutral. In the end, we failed, but this led to the development of a pro-life member community within the organization, which has had some successes through the years.

Have we stood up against unrighteousness? Yes. Have we stood firm against falsehoods? Yes. Have we mobilized others to testify on our side of various policies? Yes. Have we appealed to organizational leaders when we felt marginalized or unheard? Yes. Did we lose control, curse at others, and break other people's property? No.

There was a leader in this organization named Dennis Salisbury, MD, who had a statement read at the national meeting when he was dying of cancer in 2019. He challenged individuals on the opposite sides of contentious topics to sit down and "get coffee with" each other. I have had several such coffee conversations over the years, including breakfast with a physician who performs abortions after the first trimester. Although we disagreed on several points, we had a respectful conversation. This past session, our pro-life group caucused with several other pro-abortion delegations to develop compromise language for a resolution that concerned us greatly. After seeing our side of the discussion, concessions were made. In a world that is so polarized today, I was unsure whether such collegial discussions were possible. God proved me wrong. But what does it take? We must remember that, with the indwelling Holy Spirit, we have all the self-control, peace, patience, and love that we need to keep our cool so the Holy Spirit can lead us toward the high road. Yes, we must stand up to injustice. But if anger is our guide, we will miss the "gentle whisper" mentioned in 1 Kings 19:12b.

I have spent a lot of time meditating on the "feet fitted with the gospel of peace" part of the armor of God (Ephesians 6:15). As I wrote in my blog, *Accepting the Maybe*, "Talk Where Your Feet Are Walking You," your feet are what take you places. They are what carry around your helmet of salvation, breastplate of righteousness, shield of faith, and belt of truth. And they are what take your mouth to places so that you can breathe life into people with the Word of God. The problem is that our feet are often on a path that leads in the opposite direction of peace.

We cannot assume that everyone who enters our paths will be walking with integrity. But we should ensure we are doing so ourselves. I believe we will have a greater chance of peace if we try to find the good in those around us and genuinely listen to their position. And we need to trust that God will work all things for good, regardless of the actions of other people. We cannot let our mouths speak poison! James 3:8 makes it clear that it would be a "restless evil" and certainly is not befitting of God's people.

In my blog "The Search for Integrity in Uncomfortable Places," I wrote of a time when I was the lone dissenting voice during a board of directors vote at an organization in which I served. I was called back to a private meeting with the executive leaders, and I was nervous. Yet, they also brought peace to the meeting, and a genuine interest in understanding my position. I recognize not everyone with whom we disagree has that same level of integrity, but I have seen tensions defused once individuals are given the opportunity to genuinely feel heard.

Ecclesiastes 12:14 says, “For God will bring every deed into judgment, including every hidden thing, whether it is good or evil.” God is the judge, not us. Our job is to obey as we are called to do so, with the Holy Spirit in charge of our actions. Standing up against unrighteousness does not require yelling, violence, or destroyed property. The devil will lure us into this if we are not careful. Don’t hold onto your anger! The Bible declares that anger is a foothold the devil uses in our lives (Ephesians 4:27). You must return to more wholesome thoughts, such as those in Philippians 4:8. Put your thoughts to the test! Are they true, noble, right, pure, lovely, admirable, excellent, or praiseworthy? We are not called to turn over tables in the temple; we are called to listen to the Holy Spirit and do what He says. And often this requires forgiving and showing compassion to our neighbor.

V

Spiritual Warfare in Chronic Disease and Burnout

In this final section, we look at how these spiritual battles manifest in specific medical conditions. While medicine is often necessary, the spiritual battle in these areas is often overlooked. We'll look closely at the "hooks" of unbelief—guilt, pride, and unforgiveness—as well as the enemy's tactics of deception, temptation, and condemnation. Remember, the enemy often speaks in the first person, using "I" statements to disguise his voice as your own. When your thoughts run contrary to your new nature, there is usually an enemy behind them, and deception is one of his primary strategies. As you read, reflect on the liberating truth statements that will help you stand firm against his schemes.

CHAPTER 13

ANXIETY

Common lies: "I can't help but worry." "I've always been a worrier."
Common hooks: Unbelief, Pride
Common Tactics: Deception, Condemnation

We live in a world full of anxiety. We worry about money, our kids, and the government. We worry about our job. We worry about everything. Yet Jesus' words in Matthew 6:25-34 make it clear that we are not to worry.

> [25]*"Therefore I tell you, do not worry about your life, what you will eat or drink; or about your body, what you will wear. Is not life more important than food, and the body more important than clothes?*[26]*Look at the birds of the air; they do not sow or reap or store away in barns, and yet your heavenly Father feeds them. Are you not much more valuable than they?*[27]*Who of you by worrying can add a single hour to his life?*

He goes on to mention how much God takes care of the lilies and the grass in the field, then says,

"Therefore do not worry about tomorrow, for tomorrow will worry about itself. Each day has enough trouble of its own (v. 34)."

If simply saying "don't worry" were enough, that would be simple. Yet avoidance of worry requires discipline. There are times when that charge seems impossible.

When my son was 13 years old, he went on a two-week mission trip to a developing country on the other end of the earth. How was I, his mother, to get any rest at night?

If I did not take control of my thoughts, you could imagine where they might have traveled. What if he gets sick? What if he gets lost? What if he gets abducted? What if, what if, what if! As Stone and Gregory quote their friend, Bill Hodge, in *The Rest of the Gospel,* "The devil's favorite word is *if.*" This word can introduce much worry in God's people.

I am convinced there are only a few steps of "what ifs" until a full-blown panic attack ensues. Instead, I had to focus on the truth.

1. My son is with his father, who is the ultimate sheepdog. There has never been a time with my husband anywhere that I did not feel adequately protected.
2. It was a karate mission trip, and my son was surrounded by black belts.

3. The Filipino people love Americans, and there are no national advisories about abductions.
4. They are supporting a local martial arts ministry, and the locals know where healthcare can be found if needed.
5. I am a doctor, and I can FaceTime him with any medical needs he or the team may have and direct them on what to do.

Focusing on these truths kept me at peace, and I never lost sleep at night. I was always happy to hear from them and learn they were well, but I went on with my normal activities.

It is in times of stress and uncertainty that we must stay vigilant with our thought life. I recall being a young mother and worrying about my children. My husband and I had been infertile for three and a half years before conceiving our daughter, and her life was precious and wonderful. Yet after that journey of infertility, it was easy to be nervous about her health. I used to pray at my children's bedside every night, "God *please* keep them safe. *Please* keep them safe." After watching the movie *Courageous,* where the main character's daughter died in a car crash, I came to realize how my prayers for safety were drawn from a lack of faith. Is God big enough to get me through their death, should that occur? Yes, He is. I pray He never tests me, yet I know this to be true. My prayers started changing to "Thank you for another day." I either trust God with their lives or I don't, and I made the choice to trust Him.

I'm not saying this is easy, yet after you have experienced an episode of severe anxiety, it is wise to spend some time after calming down to analyze what thought first took you "off the rails." Usually, one worried thought carries to another, and rather than repeat this time after time, it is wise to seek a good friend or therapist to help you deconstruct your thoughts so you can see which one started the whole process. The devil knows what that is, and he will try to keep it from you. Spend time in prayerful reflection to identify it. Then seek the truth statements that counter it to disarm the enemy.

As I stated at the very beginning of this book, there are individuals who do not make enough neurotransmitters in their brains to stabilize their mood. This is a medical condition that responds quite well to medication therapy. Some people truly need medications to get them back on a level playing field with the enemy so they are able to stand firm. If you think of anxiety as an emotional elevator, with 10 being a full-blown panic attack, it is important to ensure your anxiety level lives below a three most of the time. If you live at a six or seven, you don't have much wiggle room to use the faith-based strategies I recommend in this chapter. Medications can help lower that, and too many people avoid taking them.

I had a patient named Brad who was an amazing ICU nurse. He crossed every t, and dotted every i. I worked with him while I was in training, and he never called with petty questions. He knew his stuff, and he knew his patients. If he had a question, you gave him good attention and answered it. Many healthcare professionals have obsessive-compulsive tendencies, which, in moderation, is a very good thing for patients. When patients' lives are at stake, it is good to double-check your measurements, calculations, and medication lists. Brad was a fantastic nurse.

However, when Brad retired, he did not have an outlet for this anxiety. Many couples face transition challenges at this stage of life, but it seemed clear that his anxiety was much more than typical transition issues. I started him on a medication, and I will never forget what he said to me when he came back to the clinic.

"This is what calm is? I have lived my whole life and never knew what calm was."

I realize this is a spiritual warfare book, but I cannot stress enough the importance of ensuring treatment occurs for those with true neurotransmitter brain imbalances. I believe the devil works hard to convince people not to take medications when it truly benefits them. "You need to have more faith." "You are just too weak—toughen up!" "You have a character flaw." I have told Brad's story to many people in my career to combat the devil's lies. People with these problems who refuse to take medication are selling themselves short.

Once we get on a level playing field with the enemy, we are more successful in getting control of our thoughts. This makes it much easier to tune into the "Spirit Channel" discussed in Chapter 8 and find true peace.

Trauma

Common lies: "I can never put this behind me." "I must have justice to move on."
Common hooks: Unforgiveness, Guilt
Common tactics: Condemnation, Deception

Trauma can come in many forms, including car accidents, personal assaults, extreme weather events, or any other type of accident. Biochemically, this is a huge jolt to the brain. The brain is an amoral data-processing center, which functions as part of the whole body with a common task of self-preservation. This is why the brain is involved in making you hungry when you have not eaten, or thirsty when you are getting dehydrated. If you were attacked in a dark alley, your brain will make you more hypervigilant when in dark alleys in the future. If you had a car accident at the stop sign by your house, your brain will make you more careful when you approach that intersection in the future. This is a normal and appropriate brain response, and when moderated, it is helpful.

However, the devil will exploit this. A fear of one intersection could turn into a fear of all intersections, or of driving in general. This is an overzealous and unhealthy response. As Christians with the indwelling Holy Spirit, we have all the fruit of the Spirit, including peace and faithfulness. The peaceful and faithful response is to get back behind the wheel and use the vehicle to take care of the daily business for your family, the community, and Christ. Of course, the devil wants you to do none of that, so he sends negative statements such as "driving is not safe," "you are not a good driver," "you are unsafe to be on the road," and a host of other things to keep you in bondage. Most of the time this is not true. And most of these thoughts do not originate from you.

Assaults are horrible. Having another individual, sometimes a trusted adult or family member, take advantage of or personally harm another person is a despicable act. Yet Neil Anderson believes that people are not in bondage to the things that happened to them in the past; they are in bondage to the *lies they believe* about what happened to them in the past. And these lies come straight from dark forces.

Does being assaulted or abused mean that all humans are untrustworthy? Does it mean that God is absent in your life? Does it mean that God intended to punish you? Does it mean that you are not good enough? All of these are lies straight from the enemy, and you don't have to believe them anymore.

Matthew West shared one of his fans' stories in his song "Moved by Mercy," sung as a duet where West assumes the God role and Caitlin Evanson portrays the injured individual. The song starts by narrating his fan's story of ongoing nightmares and difficulty breaking free from her past. As I listen to the bridge of that song, I imagine a final battle for the injured individual, where the devil is dragging her back with claims of unworthiness and shame, and God is pulling her in with love and mercy.

The story behind the song confirms that she grew up with an abusive father and experienced repetitive trauma. She may have been told many times by him that she was unworthy and undeserving. Dark forces continued to deliver these lies and make her think that God had abandoned her. She later came to realize that God was with her the whole time, protected her, and would continue to see her through. Once she shook the lies, she was able to break free.

My local radio station played a clip of a person telling a personal story from her young childhood, when she peed in her pants. As she waited in the bathroom for the teacher, she heard a voice say, "You are not good enough," and she carried this all through childhood into her adult life. Eventually, with a good therapist, she was able to go back to that moment in the elementary school bathroom and see that Jesus was with her in that restroom, telling her she is and always has been "Good enough." Finally, she stopped believing the lie.

I have a close friend who experienced sexual abuse in childhood. This led to a host of maladaptive coping strategies, addictions, anxiety, and depression throughout much of his adult life. He eventually found a therapist who did Eye Movement Desensitization Reprocessing therapy (EMDR), which is a psychotherapy that connects a person's recollection of a traumatic event to physical maneuvers such as intentional side-to-side eye movements or finger tapping. EMDR is thought to be one of the most effective therapies for healing past trauma. My patients have had mixed benefits from it through the years, but it worked well for my friend. His explanation was priceless: "I was able to go back in time and rescue that little boy." In short, he went back to that horrible event and reprocessed how he felt about it. He was no longer in bondage to the false beliefs he had about himself all these years. In short, he stopped believing the lie.

I have a patient who faced similar repetitive traumas in childhood. I referred her to counseling several times, but she would go only a few times and stop. She did not like that they wanted to talk about her childhood, because that is a painful place she did not wish to revisit. She participated in a spiritual warfare class in the past, but this did not help her at the time. I have been her doctor for over 20 years, but I never could figure out which painful memory had caused her bondage and made her feel so unworthy.

I once pondered how she would react if she had to stop fast at the end of a grocery aisle to avoid hitting someone coming the other way. For me, I would say, "Excuse me," and go on with my day. But she admitted she might hear terrible negative thoughts, such as, "You are an idiot, you almost hit him! He probably thinks you are stupid. Why can't you be more careful?" These are echoes of all the things her family may have told her when she was growing up. She has an amazing, loving husband and supportive children, and yet she has felt unworthy for much of her adult life. She agreed to see another therapist and had a spiritual breakthrough. When she last saw me, her anxiety and depression were surprisingly under good control. She told me that, through counseling, she finally forgave herself. It is a cruel deception when a traumatized child feels like their victimization is their own fault. She has now shaken off that lie and is in a much better emotional place. I did a literal "happy dance" for her in my exam room!

If you are someone who continues to struggle with the weight of past trauma, please understand you are a victor in Christ. You may still feel like a victim, and I don't wish to minimize your pain. Yet, try to imagine yourself as a proud silverback gorilla pounding on his chest. In Christ, you have this kind of victory!

The Holy God of the universe lives inside of you, with a full abundance of love, joy, peace, patience, kindness, goodness, faithfulness, gentleness, and self-control (Gal 5:22-23a). Victimhood may be what you are used to, and it may have been your identity for many years. You may have nursed it along with the anger and unforgiveness that came with it. You may think this is an identity that you cannot escape from, but that is a lie straight from the gates of Hell. In the past, when people did things to harm you, you were a victim. But these people are probably not directly harming you now. The harm you feel today comes from disrupted self-confidence that makes you think you are the same scared child you were back then.

Come out of that darkness! See yourself as the victor you truly are! Live in the truth that the God who rescues and saves also dwells within you. God is not a victim, so you are no longer a victim either. Don't claim that as your identity any longer!

David's Strategy for Peace

In reading the Psalms of David, one encounters a profound expression of fear, anger, worry, and grief. Though David was anointed by Samuel as the future king of Israel and spent his early years in service to King Saul, his relationship with Saul later soured. Saul, threatened by David's military success and growing popularity, embarked on a ruthless campaign to kill him. David, who had done nothing to deserve this, found himself on the run, often hiding in caves while Saul's army pursued him. During this time, David wrote many beautiful psalms, pouring out his emotions and fears to God.

Psalm 59 is one such psalm. The first 15 verses are filled with fear and anger, yet the tone shifts dramatically at the end:

But as for me, I will sing about your power.

Each morning I will sing with joy about your unfailing love.

For you have been my refuge,

a place of safety when I am in distress.

O my Strength, to you I sing praises,

for you, O God, are my refuge,

the God who shows me unfailing love.

(Psalm 59:16-17, NLT)

His pleading turned to praise, his praise turned into trust, and his trust turned into peace. There have been times in my life when I was anxious about things, and I told myself that I need to trust God more. "I am not getting out of this chair until I trust God!" However, I am not likely to trust God through mere stubbornness. David figured out the secret.

Psalm 8:3-4 (NLT)

When I look at the night sky and see the work of your fingers—

The moon and the stars you set in place—

What are mere mortals that you should think about them,

Human beings that you should care for them."

In Psalm 9, David recounts how God saved him from his enemies, and trusts that God will do it again. In Psalm 16:8 he says, "I know the Lord is always with me. I will not be shaken, for he is right beside me (NLT)." I believe that the path to peace in times of stress often looks like this:

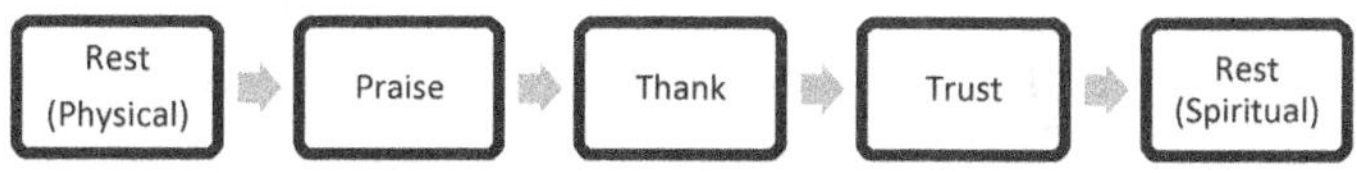

Our bodies need physical rest. I have counseled numerous patients over the years who desire a medication to help them sleep, yet when I explore further I find they are way too busy, working long hours, volunteering too much, and trying to be "all things to all people." Medications work poorly when we have way too much to do. Sometimes the path to spiritual rest starts with giving ourselves enough time for physical rest.

I once had a patient who came to me with problems sleeping. Upon review, she was not clinically depressed or anxious; she was simply too busy. She worked full-time, volunteered at her child's school, and was a soccer mom in charge of the team fundraiser. Weekends were packed with sporting events, leaving no time for rest. While she was lying in bed at night, her mind was busy with all the things she needed to do the next day, making it hard to wind down. While I can offer a medication to sedate her, the real cure is to take some things off her plate, and I don't have a pill for that.

Not long after, she fell and broke her leg. She required surgery and was in a wheelchair for a while. A lot of the things she had been responsible for had to be handed over to someone else. I'm not saying that God broke her leg, but I suspect He used this to reset her priorities. The devil will often try to get us overly busy, diluting our impact on one or more self-assigned tasks, to make us less effective or simply make us miserable. *The Parable of the Talents* in Matthew 25 makes it clear that we are not to "bury our talents," but to use them for Christ and His glory. But sometimes the things we busy ourselves with are not from God's direction, but "other stuff" the world uses to distract us.

I have a classic Type A, driven personality. We never had any money when I was growing up, so I wanted to give my kids all the experiences I couldn't have when I was their age. On Tuesdays, we had school, piano practice, gymnastics, and then karate. Why did I think it was a wise idea to pack so much into one evening? No wonder I was stressed out when my kids were little. Suffice it to say that I eventually came to my senses and admitted that this was simply too much.

Once we decompress our schedule and get some physical rest, then we can truly focus on listening to the Spirit.

First Kings, Chapters 18 and 19, tell the story of Elijah. In Chapter 18, he challenged the prophets of the pagan god, Baal, to a contest. They created two altars with sacrifices, and Elijah challenged them to pray hard to Baal to make the sacrifice catch fire with divine intervention. Four hundred and fifty prophets of Baal were praying to their fake god all day, and nothing happened. Then Elijah told the people to flood his sacrifice with water three times to ensure it was saturated. He prayed to the real God, and fire consumed the sacrifice, "and also licked up the water in the trench (1 Kings 18:38)." The people fell prostrate, declaring, "The Lord—he is God" (v. 39)! Elijah commanded them to seize and kill the prophets of Baal. What a wonderful victory this was for God and his prophet!

However, the king's wife, Jezebel, was furious about the death of the prophets, and she sent many after Elijah to kill him. Elijah ran for his life for over a day and eventually said, "I have had enough, Lord. Take my life; I am no better than my ancestors (v.4)." Then he did something that his mortal body needed. "He lay down under the tree and fell asleep. (v. 5)." Angels came to attend to his physical needs for food and water saying, "Get up and eat, for the journey is too much for you. (v. 7)." After meeting his physical needs for rest and food, he was strengthened to continue his journey.

As you face worries in your life, start by getting some physical rest. Then, thank and praise God for how He has sustained you in the past. You may find that trust and spiritual rest follow naturally. When we begin to thank God for the good things in our lives, the tone of our worries changes. Our focus shifts from anxiety to the true source of peace. As we praise God in our hearts, we inevitably remember His power and love. This leads to trust, and trust leads to spiritual rest.

CHAPTER 14

DEPRESSION

Common lies: "I'm no good." "Nobody cares about me." "I don't matter."
Common hook: Guilt
Common Tactics: Condemnation, Deception

Not all depression is caused by spiritual warfare. However, the forces of evil will often attack us where we are most vulnerable.

As with anxiety, some depression is truly biological, with an imbalance of brain neurochemistry that needs to be fixed. Just like high blood pressure, diabetes, and thyroid disease need medication, depression does as well. To do anything less is to sell ourselves short. Our culture needs to push past the stigma of behavioral health disease management to allow this to occur earlier in clinical disease processes. In patients with true neurochemical imbalances, spiritual warfare is an adjunctive treatment only, not the primary one.

Yet, as I mentioned, dark spiritual forces will attack wherever they can, especially at our weakest moments.

Moments of intense stress

Jesus experienced extreme stress while he was tempted for 40 days in the desert. Luke 4:1-8 recounts this story.

> *Jesus, full of the Holy Spirit, left the Jordan and was led by the Spirit into the wilderness, where for forty days he was tempted by the devil. He ate nothing during those days, and at the end of them he was hungry.*
>
> *The devil said to him, "If you are the Son of God, tell this stone to become bread."*
>
> *Jesus answered, "It is written: 'Man shall not live on bread alone.'"*
>
> *The devil led him up to a high place and showed him in an instant all the kingdoms of the world. And he said to him, "I will give you all their authority and splendor; it has been given to me, and I can give it to anyone I want to. If you worship me, it will all be yours."*
>
> *Jesus answered, "It is written: 'Worship the Lord your God and serve him only.'"*

The devil saw Jesus at one of his weakest moments and tried to take advantage of it. He will do the same with you.

Consider the times when we are having a bad day. We lose our keys. The car won't start. We are hit with a new deadline at work. Our kids roll their eyes at us. Our ailing parents do not take our advice. All of these things can put us in a "funk," and the devil will take advantage of it.

Be watchful for globalizing statements in your head. "My work is *always* this bad." "My kids *always* disrespect me." "This day has gone to the dogs, and there is nothing I can do about it." I have heard this called "stinkin' thinkin.'" But recognize that, in Christ, this is not our nature, so if we are in these negative thought spirals, we probably have spiritual forces luring us there.

Our struggles with depressive thoughts would be easier if we kept our eyes focused on Jesus. On our Christian walk, our goal is to keep our eyes fixed on Jesus at the end of the road and deflect our attention away from the demons in the windows. Matthew Chapter 14 recounts the time when Jesus walked on the water towards his disciples in the middle of the storm on the Sea of Galilee. In an initial amazing act of faith, Peter walked out toward him on the water. However, shortly thereafter, he turned his attention to the wind, and he sank like a rock. We face the same peril when we focus our attention on the storms in our lives rather than on the Savior.

With each interaction during Jesus' temptation in the desert, the devil misused scripture, but Jesus was not to be fooled. In *The Rest of the Gospel* by Dan Stone and David Gregory, they speak of "The Line," an imaginary dividing point between the heavenly realm and the physical realm. As Christians, our spirit is in heaven right now, but our soul and body exist in the physical realm, subject to worldly forces. When Jesus was born on this earth, his body and soul were in the physical realm with us. His Spirit was also above the line like ours, but he was able to focus his soul above the line in all things. And for this reason, the devil failed to tempt Jesus away from scriptural truth.

In Chapter 8, we reviewed our Spirit, Soul, Body diagrams. It is in our best interest to keep our souls turned toward the spirit, rather than toward the world. This is the best way to tune in to the spirit channel, our primary source of truth, rather than to outward noises.

In continuing the story of Elijah introduced in the last chapter, 1 Kings 19 goes on to say that, after being refreshed by the angels, Elijah traveled forty days until he reached Horeb, the mountain of God.

> *The Lord said, "Go out and stand on the mountain in the presence of the Lord, for the Lord is about to pass by."*
>
> *Then a great and powerful wind tore the mountains apart and shattered the rocks before the Lord, but the Lord was*

not in the wind. After the wind there was an earthquake, but the Lord was not in the earthquake. After the earthquake came a fire, but the Lord was not in the fire. And after the fire came a gentle whisper. When Elijah heard it, he pulled his cloak over his face and went out and stood at the mouth of the cave.

Then a voice said to him, "What are you doing here, Elijah?" (Vs. 11-13)

The Lord's message was not in the wind, earthquake, or fire; it was in the "gentle whisper." If we want to hear the Spirit, we have to be attentively listening. If our soul is faced outward towards the world, this will be much more difficult to do.

Bereavement

People often struggle with sadness following the death of a loved one. Such feelings are natural and expected. Even Jesus wept when he saw the suffering of Mary and Martha after Lazarus' death (John 11:35). It is appropriate and normal to feel sad and to miss the presence of the departed person. There is nothing shameful about shedding tears in this circumstance. Grief should not be rushed, and individual people experience it differently. Some are ready to clean out closets right away, and others keep these things around as token memories for a long time.

Elisabeth Kübler-Ross is well known for her "5 Stages of Grief" model, which includes denial, anger, bargaining, depression, and acceptance. While her initial work was studying people given terminal diagnoses, this model has been widely applied to grief from many causes. This is not intended to be a linear model, since people will move between stages or revisit stages from time to time. Yet it is helpful to validate what patients are feeling and recognize these stages as a common and normal experience for most.

Yet, at each stage, there is an opportunity for the devil to make things worse. When people become bitter and unforgiving about a death, it sours them and introduces a "bitter root" as we discussed in Chapter 12. The devil will try to globalize our feelings of sadness, saying, "My life will never be good again," or "I can never live a happy life again." These thoughts are not helpful.

In *The Rest of the Gospel,* Dan Stone and David Gregory have a chapter called "The Gift of Misery" in which they say, "Thank God for your misery. It prepares you to be a vessel for His use, for His strength—not yours—to flow through...In your weakness is your strength. In your misery is your hope. In your death is your life. In your nothing is His everything."

Dan Stone was serious about this. In an earlier chapter of that book, he shared his own personal struggle with grief after losing his wife. He lived from his spirit, but in times when he grieved for her, he would step down into his soul and stay there a while. He would miss her and the things they did together. But after a while, he would return his focus to his spirit and say, "God, all things are of you. I enjoyed that little party. My soul appreciated that. But I am a spiritual being. And everything is all right" (p. 139).

The devil will try to keep you in those negative thoughts as long as possible. As we turn our soul back to our spiritual core, we will endure grief more effectively.

Suicidal Thoughts

I am convinced that the devil is behind many suicidal thoughts experienced by individuals. As a born-again child of God with the indwelling Holy Spirit, you have the full measure of peace, joy, thankfulness, and self-control. Yet sadly, many Christians still suffer from suicidal thoughts. Even more sadly, many act on them and succeed. We should not think any of us, even pastors, are immune to these attacks. They are, quite simply, from the enemy.

The final stage of Jesus' temptation is recorded in Luke 4:9-12.

> *The devil led him to Jerusalem and had him stand on the highest point of the temple. "If you are the Son of God," he said, "throw yourself down from here. For it is written:*

"He will command his angels concerning you to guard you carefully; they will lift you up in their hands, so that you will not strike your foot against a stone.'"

Jesus answered, "It is said: 'Do not put the Lord your God to the test.'"

When Jesus came to earth, He was fully man. He had physical needs for food, water, and shelter like the rest of us. When he was whipped, had thorns driven into his scalp, and was nailed, he bled. When he was speared and suffocated on the cross, he died.

During Jesus's temptation in the desert, his time for death had not yet come. But considering what we know about the physical laws of the universe, jumping as a man from the highest point in the temple is a terrible idea. Jesus had enough faith to avoid manipulation from the devil. Yet, in my opinion, this story demonstrates that the devil has been in the suicide business a long time.

Luke 4:13 goes on to say, "When the devil had finished all this tempting, he left him until an opportune time." This means that the devil was not through with Jesus, nor is he ever through with us. But as we follow Jesus' example, keeping our souls focused on our indwelling spirit, the devil's noise will be less audible.

Victory Story

One of my patients, Becky, reached out to me for advice about her daughter, who lived in another city and was struggling with depression and suicidal thoughts. While the daughter lived outside of my standard referral area, Becky asked for general advice on how to find a good psychiatrist and how to keep her daughter safe. I provided this help as best I could.

Not long after that, Becky came to my clinic for her own appointment. Remembering the stress with her daughter, I asked Becky to complete a depression and anxiety questionnaire. For each question, the scale is 0-3, with 0 being the best and 3 being the worst. Surprisingly, her questionnaires had zeros straight down the page.

I asked several follow-up questions to establish the accuracy of the questionnaires, and it was clear that she was doing well despite her daughter's situation. Becky's daughter was still not well. She was still depressed, in bed most days, and was barely getting to work. It was unclear whether her basic physical needs were being met. Becky had offered to help her further, and the daughter declined.

Despite all of this enormous stress, Becky's depression and anxiety questionnaires were normal! How could this be? I asked her, "How did you do that?"

Becky went on to say that she had done all she could do, and at this point, she had turned her daughter over to God's hands. She still called her, offered to help, and aided where she could. But she trusted God to take care of her daughter, and this brought peace.

I wish I could say I would have the same spiritual strength as she. This does not mean that we walk away and do nothing. Becky still interjected where she could and provided support and comfort. But she also trusted in God, and He faithfully got her daughter through.

Chapter 15

Healthy Eating

Common lies: "I can't help myself." "I deserve to eat it."
Common hooks: Guilt, Pride, Unforgiveness
Common tactics: Temptation, Condemnation, Deception

Obesity

It is no secret that the United States of America has some of the worst health indicators of industrialized countries. We eat too much, exercise too little, sleep poorly, and endure too much stress. Many chronic conditions, such as hypertension and diabetes, could be vastly improved or eliminated if people would simply eat better and exercise more. Yet making this happen seems nearly impossible sometimes.

Before I begin, I affirm that obesity is a complex disease, with genetics, biology, and neurohormonal factors at play, in addition to lifestyle and habits. It is clear that the weight "set point" in some people's brains is higher than it needs to be, and I have intense empathy for this. I had a dear friend who monitored her calories, exercised with a trainer, and got sufficient sleep, but still did not lose weight. I have few words of comfort for these individuals, for their weight problems are not easily explained. Yet for many others, it is clear they eat a lot of sweets, fried foods, and processed carbohydrates, and drink way too many liquid calories.

I had another patient who was faithfully logging her calories in the same fitness app and brought it to me with the full understanding that she was hundreds of calories over each day. Her morning would often start with a 400-calorie latte from the local coffee shop. She was well aware that it was high in calories, and she knew she could hit her calorie goals much more easily if she would simply drink a non-calorie beverage. But she did it anyway, day after day. At the time, I did not have much to offer her. When faced with similar situations today, I can provide much more.

In Chapter 9, I told the story of my dear friend who quit smoking after seeing his kids "smoke" their macaroni and cheese at the dinner table. That day, he crossed a line—he was no longer a smoker trying to quit but a non-smoker who craved a cigarette. For the first time, he saw himself in the power of his new identity. The God in him was much bigger than the physical craving he experienced.

Most of us do not see the spiritual warfare that keeps us from achieving our healthcare goals. The devil will say we are not strong enough. If that does not work, he will appeal to our pride to say we deserve to have what we want. Consider the scenario of avoiding chocolate cake.

Perhaps someone is trying to eat better and avoid sweets, but starts to crave chocolate cake after seeing it on television. We might say to ourselves, "You can't have that chocolate cake. That chocolate cake is bad for you. That chocolate cake will make your diabetes worse. That chocolate cake will make you gain weight. That chocolate cake will make your cholesterol worse. For the love of all that is Holy, don't eat that chocolate cake!!" Why does this fail? Because we are still thinking of the chocolate cake!

To win the battle for health behaviors, we must win the battle for our minds. The devil wants you to eat the cake so he can condemn you after you do so. Have you ever indulged in something you were trying to avoid, only to feel guilty about it later? We engage in a lot of negative self-talk, criticizing and heaping judgment on ourselves, yet we completely miss the fact that the devil is pushing our buttons. He does not inspire all dietary indiscretions, but he will happily take advantage of them when they happen.

I don't know how many people I have had in my career say how hesitant they were to come for their visit because they thought I would be disappointed in them. I feel pained every time I hear that, because I know that is the enemy talking. Of course, the enemy wants to keep them away from the place that is trying to make them healthier. I am my patients' cheerleader, not their judge, and it is always my goal to start fresh with each visit to see what we can accomplish by next time. I never criticize my patients for bad outcomes, so why do they feel such condemning thoughts when they come for their visit? They hear these condemning thoughts in their own voice in their own head, and they don't know it is the enemy behind it.

The fruit of the Spirit includes self-control, and we learned in Chapter 9 that we gain an infinite amount of it when we are saved and receive the indwelling Holy Spirit. Yet if we don't *believe* we have self-control, then it is of no value to us. We must lift our shield of faith, choose to believe the truth, and act as if it is so. Doing anything less dooms us to failure.

Each of us is faced with numerous opportunities each day to snack and have dietary indiscretions. Unlike my friend who stopped smoking, we cannot stop eating and still live. Thus, with each meal and during snacks in between, we have the opportunity for temptation.

Philippians 4:8 reminds us to think wholesome thoughts that are true, noble, admirable, and praiseworthy. It is true that high sugars and processed carbs will make us feel tired once the sugar rush wears off. It is true that we will feel better if we eat better. It is noble to treat our body as a temple. It is admirable and praiseworthy to stand firm against temptation. Remember the Christian walk analogy discussed in Chapter 5. Our goal is to keep our eyes on the truth and away from the things we see in the windows.

There are some practical ways to make this easier. Meal prepping sounds like a lot of work, but it actually saves time and money in the long run. Do you cook dinner a few times per week? If so, it does not take much more time to cook extra. Invest in some single-serving glass storage containers and make lunches for the week. Consider how much time you spend sitting in restaurant drive-throughs or standing in line at the cafeteria. All of this time could be eliminated if some of it were invested in the meal prep day.

If you know you shouldn't eat it, don't buy it! If someone in your house buys it, have them store it in their bedroom or tucked away in a cabinet so it is out of sight. Ephesians 4:27 reminds us not to give the devil a foothold. Having junk food in your house is a simple invitation to eat more junk.

Experiment with healthy snacks. Perhaps you are accustomed to eating chips, crackers, and sweets, but you may find that you can equally enjoy other, more wholesome options if you give them a try. Most people do well if they focus on fresh fruits, vegetables, and protein sources.

Do a sugar detox. I personally have struggled with chronic hives triggered by my thyroid condition, and I have tried a few dietary experiments over the years to see if I could reduce my symptoms. Once, I tried the Whole30 diet, which avoids all processed carbohydrates, sugars, and dairy. Not adding sweetened creamers to my coffee was tough. I had a lot of fatigue that first week, but by week two this had resolved. Because many of my regular foods were not allowed, I experimented with other vegetables and came to learn that I absolutely love roasted Brussels sprouts and butternut squash. My hives did not benefit, so I decided to stop the diet after the fourth week, and I looked forward to my first day with coffee creamer. To my surprise, the coffee was much too sweet! My taste buds had reset, and I wasn't aware of it until the diet was over.

Before this diet, I ate flavored yogurt. Once, I had purchased plain yogurt by accident and found it bitter and disgusting. Yet now, I absolutely love it. I add a little bit of coconut flakes to give it some texture and a tiny bit of sweetness, and I'm a happy lady. I would have never tolerated this before the sugar detox from the Whole30 diet.

One of my aunts got diagnosed with diabetes, and she stopped eating sweets. Once she stopped eating sugar, she found she did not crave it anymore. I realize this is not the case for everyone, and sugar is absolutely addictive for some people. But I think it is also true that we could retrain our taste buds if we simply gave it a try.

If, while reading this, you hear things like, "I could never do that," or "That could never work for me," consider where these thoughts are coming from. The tempter wants to take your daily victory, and he feeds these lies to us on a regular basis. The truth is that these strategies have worked for many people before you, and they could probably work for you, too.

You are not hopelessly trying to eat better; you are the bride of Christ with his power inside of you. Stop spending so much time peering in the apartment complex windows. Get back to the middle of the road and put your eyes back on Jesus. He is all the strength you need.

Eating Disorders

The devil also has his hand in eating disorders such as anorexia and bulimia. Anorexia is a condition where people do not eat enough calories. Bulimia is a condition where people usually eat plenty, sometimes to excess, which we label *bingeing*, but later engage in forced vomiting and laxative abuse, which we call *purging*. Many times, these individuals will go into a many-month treatment program yet still struggle with their maladaptive thoughts about food. Hopefully, now that you have gotten to this stage in the book, you realize that demons are likely at play in some of these situations.

One of the first famous deaths from anorexia was Karen Carpenter, a singer and drummer from the 1970s and early 1980s. She sang with her brother as The Carpenters, creating 17 top 20 hits, 10 gold singles, nine gold albums, and one mini-platinum album, and earning three Grammy awards. A 2010 article from The Guardian summarizes her tragic story (Schmidt, 2010). What started as a simple diet to look more attractive led to abuse of laxatives and vomiting-inducing agents, layered clothing to hide her thin frame, and mealtime practices of sharing her food with others to make her look like she was eating more of it. Prior to her death, she had regained some weight and was seeming more healthy, but was found dead at home. The listed cause of death was "emetine cardiotoxicity due to or as a consequence of anorexia nervosa." In short, the medication she was taking to induce vomiting, ipecac, killed her.

The National Eating Disorders Association reports that 9% or 30 million Americans will have an eating disorder in their lifetime (Bunnell, 2025). The global eating disorder prevalence increased from 3.5% to 7.8% between 2000 and 2018, and 22% of children and adolescents worldwide show disordered eating. Eating disorders have the second-highest mortality rate of any psychiatric illness behind opiate addiction, and every 52 minutes someone dies as a direct consequence of an eating disorder. Despite improvements in treatment, incidence rates keep rising. I am confident that some of these cases are triggered by spiritual deception.

And yet, there are winners. I am so proud of my patient, Chloe. She struggled with anorexia for years but has maintained herself at a reasonable weight for over two years. Her problem with anorexia began after she experienced a severe illness that lasted over a year. Thankfully, she had a full physical recovery, but the emotional wounds were long-lasting.

She began to eat healthy and exercise, but this eventually became too extreme. Her excessively healthy diet led to insufficient calorie intake. Unlike most people with anorexia, she truly did want to gain more weight, and she knew she would be healthier if she did so, but she simply had barriers with getting enough calories in her system. Chloe resisted the diagnosis of anorexia for a long time, concerned about the social implications and feeling she could manage it herself. She had had a very supportive network, which was reassuring. She did successfully gain some weight, but she still had metabolic abnormalities.

Thankfully, with the help of a counselor and an athletic trainer, she has now maintained her weight at a healthier level for two years. The interesting thing about Chloe's case is that she truly did want to regain weight. This is not the case with many other patients with her condition.

It is hard to imagine the condemning thoughts individuals with eating disorders are hearing and the spiritual abuse they undergo. With bulimia, they have strong temptations to eat. Then once they eat it (binge), they face condemning thoughts which drive them to induce vomiting or take laxatives (purge).

As we remember the Christian walk analogy from Chapter 5, bulimic patients are lured to the window and tempted with the fruits they see. Then once they partake, they are pummeled with condemning thoughts and further enticed to abuse their physical bodies with purging. Once they purge, they may have short-term relief, only to later feel condemning thoughts about having done the purge activities.

If we keep treating these patients as though these condemning thoughts are their own, they may continue to feel hopeless about overcoming them. They will never recognize another source rooted in the "rulers," "authorities," or "spiritual forces of evil in the heavenly realms" which Ephesians 6:12 declares. The devil's goal is to always work in the shadows, making people think he is not there. And as long as the patient considers that the condemning thoughts are theirs alone, they will never receive the tools to stand firm against the enemy.

Chloe is a Christian, so she and I had conversations about spiritual warfare and her authority in Christ to tell the enemy to flee. Her dietitian/counselor and her athletic trainer, who see her regularly, carry the greatest influence and receive more credit than I for her success. But I think there was value in her being reminded that she has authority in Christ. Our job is not to fight the battle that Jesus already won. Our job is to remember that God is so much bigger than the devil, and *He lives in us*! The enemy is trapped behind those apartment windows and cannot touch us. Once we recognize *and truly believe* that we have the authority to ignore him, doing so becomes much easier.

CHAPTER 16

EXERCISE

Common lies: "I don't need to exercise." "I am too tired to exercise."
Common Hooks: Pride, Unbelief
Common tactics: Deception

The industrial revolution, modern transportation, and digital technologies make it easier to earn an income with little or no exercise built into our day. I struggle with this myself, as my executive position four days per week has me behind a computer for most of the day. If exercise is to occur, I must proactively make it happen.

Exercise improves not only our stamina and physical health, but also our emotional and spiritual health. Study after study continues to show this, so much so that I sometimes question why we feel we need to keep studying it! We sleep better and have more energy if we exercise. Yet the catch-22 is that we sometimes feel too tired to exercise.

Lots of patients over the years tell me that they know they should exercise, but they are so tired after they come home from work that they cannot do so. For those patients who work on their feet all day or do manual labor, this comment may be justified. Some of the hospital nurses I treat get over 10,000 steps per day with their normal work routine. They are already hitting their move goals by simply being at work, and for them, the excuse may be valid. Yet most of my patients have sedentary jobs, and this sedentary behavior is *making them tired.* And while it seems counterintuitive, the best way to fix the tiredness is to exercise.

I practice in Texas, where it is hot much of the year. Many people tell me it is too hot to exercise, and admittedly, it is still 80 degrees sometimes at dusk and dawn. But we cannot allow ourselves to avoid all exercise due to the heat alone. Start with five minutes and see how it goes. Then move up to 10, then 15, then 20.

It's amazing how much some people's mental health improves if they simply go outside. One of my family members would sometimes have a sad, depressed day, sometimes for no good reason. The solution was not to lie in bed all day feeling sorry for herself, but to go outside. Within ten minutes, she would often perk up and feel much better.

From a spiritual warfare perspective, consider what was happening. She felt sad and blue for no specific reason. Who was telling her to stay in her funk? Who was telling her to lie around the house? Who was telling her that the day was bad and there was nothing she could do about it? That "who" was the enemy. Getting her out of bed and outside in nature distracted her with flowers, butterflies, and clouds. In short, it took the devil off his game and got her mind focused on good things in the world that she enjoys and that God created. The devil can't do good work in that atmosphere.

When exercising outside is not an option, then indoor exercise can still be helpful. But exercise must be planned, not an afterthought. Too many people approach exercise with the philosophy, "If I feel good today, then I will exercise." Yet it is regular exercise that makes us feel good, and the devil does not want you to remember that. So he dishes the lie to you that you don't feel good enough to exercise, so you don't exercise, and you continue to feel bad. And he just sits back and laughs.

There are many exercise "hacks" I have shared with patients over the years. Park farther away from building entrances. Take the stairs instead of the elevator. Stand up and stretch every hour. On breaks, take a little walk. There are under-the-desk pedal bikes that some can use for exercise. I personally have a standing desk with a walking pad, with which I get about 8,000 to10,000 steps per day.

Resistance exercises once or twice per week are a good idea, too. As you selectively strengthen muscles with exercise bands, squats, or weightlifting, you strengthen your bones and train your muscles to be even more efficient with exercise. I tell my patients that I am not trying to turn anyone into an Olympic athlete or supermodel; I just want them to be healthy. I want them to be able to do the same things in ten years that they can do today, and the best way to ensure that is with regular exercise.

I encourage my patients to start somewhere and build up from there. I had a former classmate who sometimes would dread doing her morning walk, but she would tell herself to just go outside for two minutes. If she still didn't want to do it, she could come back home, but that never happened. Once she got up, got moving, and went outside, the motivation to continue became easier. This can also be true with indoor exercise and resistance training. Once you fight back against the negative thoughts and focus on the truth, you again take the devil off his game and may even find you enjoyed exercising after all.

Some people have joint and back pain that limits their mobility, and I have much empathy for these individuals. But too often, I have seen the spiral of disability happen in front of me, which looks like this:

My knee hurts, so I don't exercise.

The muscles around my knee get weak.

The knee joint has less support.

The knee hurts more.

I exercise less.

The muscles around the knee get weaker.

The knee joint has less support.

The knee hurts more….etc.

This graphic displays it well.

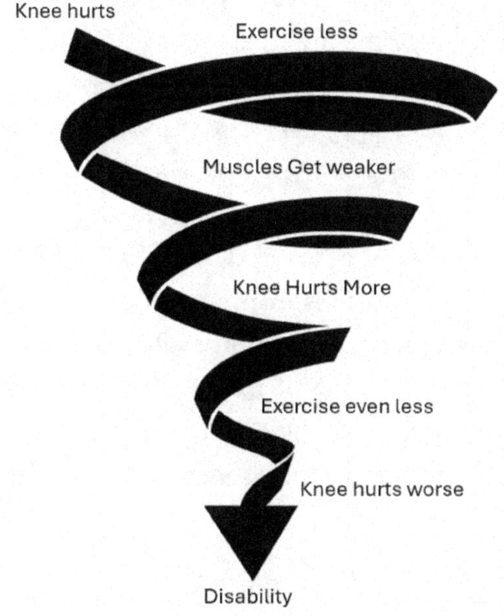

What can someone do when they have pain that limits them? There are numerous videos available online for chair exercises, tai chi, and yoga. Don't neglect exercising the rest of your body when only one or two parts are ailing you. The belief that you cannot exercise at all is straight from the enemy himself. Water exercise is an excellent option for many who have access to a pool. There is good data that simply walking along the bottom of the pool is helpful, or joining a water exercise class. Floating on a pool noodle doesn't do much, however. Don't let the devil trick you into thinking that floating or sitting in the water is "exercise."

I have had patients over the years get despondent because they lose the ability to do certain things that they wish they could still do, and all too often they emotionally "give up." *Patients who spend their time being grateful for what they can still do, and doing it, fare much better than those who spend their time being bitter about the things they can no longer do.* We learned in Chapter 7 where bitterness actually comes from. As a Christian, you are a new creation with the indwelling Holy Spirit. Bitterness is not a fruit of the Spirit, so bitterness is not coming from you. The sooner we realize this is an attack from the enemy, the sooner we can call him out and stand firm against him.

The local Tyler Area Senior Citizens' Center used to have a slogan which said, "People do not stop doing things because they get old. They get old because they stop doing things." It is true that our body is temporary, has injuries, and contains organs that eventually fail. Most people at age 60 can't do what they used to do at age 20. But we should do as much as we can for as long as we can do it safely. We are not as fragile or broken as the enemy sometimes leads us to believe.

Don't use fatigue, pain, or disability as an excuse to avoid doing the exercise of which you are still capable. If you want to be able to do the same things five years from now that you can do today, stand firm against the enemy's lies and get up and move!

CHAPTER 17

BURNOUT

Common lies: "The person I care for had a bad outcome, so I am a terrible caregiver."
Common hooks: Guilt, Pride
Common tactics: Condemnation, Deception

While this story comes from my life as a physician, the burden of feeling responsible for another person's choices is something many of us carry—whether you are a parent watching a child stray, a spouse watching a partner struggle, or a pastor watching a congregant fall. Many of us at times feel insufficient and undervalued. If you have felt this way, I assure you that you are not alone.

This chapter focuses on healthcare burnout. But if you have been the primary caregiver for an ill loved one, you may have experienced burnout yourself. In this chapter, I "peel back the curtain" to show those of you who do not work in healthcare what medical professionals experience.

This is a story I did not think I would ever share outside of close personal circles. As medical professionals, we see tragedy, give bad news, and have no room for mistakes. We are in the most regulated industry in America, and feel the weight of rules, quality metrics, coding requirements, and numerous other details day after day. It's a privilege, but it's difficult.

I had a patient I will call Taylor, who had a long-term problem with mental illness. I tried to refer him to psychiatry, but he declined due to insurance issues and personal preference. I did the best I could, adjusting medications numerous times. He had good days and bad days. It was clear that there was stress in his life that impacted his situation, which I could not fix.

Once, he returned to the clinic and admitted that things were not going well. But he had started counseling with the person with whom he had a conflict and hoped this would make things better. I offered standard safety precautions, such as removing weapons from the home and engaging with other family members for support.

There really isn't anything that can prepare someone to see their patient's face on all the headlines of the local news. My nurse reached out to me that fateful evening to let me know Taylor had been arrested for killing another individual.

I left a message for our organization's legal team the next business day. By noon, Taylor's lawyer was asking to talk to me. The feeling of failure was overwhelming. What could I have done? What should I have done? I felt like I had the dead person's blood on my hands.

In some jurisdictions, doctors have faced prosecution for the horrible things their patients do. Victim families sometimes sue. In law, conversations you have outside of your legal team are "discoverable," and friends and family can be subpoenaed to testify about any details they were told. I was scared, threatened, and disturbed. My feelings of guilt for this death were immense, but the legal team told me not to talk to anyone about anything.

Contemplate that for a moment. *Anything you say to anyone outside of your legal team could be used against you.* I wanted to speak to other colleagues to learn what I could have done differently, or be reassured that it wasn't my fault. But, during the most disparaging moment of my clinical career, I had to endure in near silence.

I continued to assist Taylor in his medical care until his death while awaiting trial. I don't know any details about how the gun fired or what truly happened, and I never will.

Several years later, I attended our health system's Board meeting, where we were getting re-educated by our legal team about the need to avoid conversations with people outside of the legal team when things go awry with patients. At that time, I could not be silent. I shared my story about Taylor and encouraged them to find a way to help healthcare workers unpack what they are feeling when things don't go well with patients. Over time, my organization created a peer coaching program that has legal protections where people can speak freely and get the reassurance they need. More organizations should do the same.

But such programs are only partly successful if we don't recognize the spiritual warfare that underpins much of burnout in the first place. Some have labeled insecurity as "imposter syndrome," which Merriam-Webster defines as "a psychological condition that is characterized by persistent doubt concerning one's abilities or accomplishments accompanied by the fear of being exposed as a fraud despite evidence of one's ongoing success." But labeling something only gets people so far. If you truly are competent, but you feel incompetent, someone is telling you to think this way, and that person is not you.

In the situation with Taylor, I had no clear evidence of an immediate threat to anyone's life, and I am not gifted with the power of prophecy. Expecting me to predict the future with clarity is a lie straight from the gates of hell. I have questioned myself with "regrets," but this is simply another form of guilt, and we already learned in Chapter 7 that guilt is one of the main tactics of the devil.

There is a powerful scene in the movie *Parkland* where the medical resident (Zac Efron) staffing the emergency room (ER) had the unbelievable burden of performing CPR on a dying president, John F. Kennedy. The attending physician was in a meeting, so this young man was left to lead the team. After a few moments of a dazed expression, he flipped on doctor mode and started barking out orders. The movie portrays him taking care of routine ER maladies later that very same day. What other profession outside of healthcare expects people to "carry on as normal" after being arm deep in a dead president's blood? There are still patients who need care in the ER, so we must go on. No wonder ER doctors have some of the highest rates of burnout and suicide.

If we are facing burnout, how do we claw our way out? Whether you are a physician navigating a tragic clinical outcome, a parent exhausted by a prodigal child, or a pastor drained by ministry demands, the answer is the same. When it is hard to hear past the cacophony of demons screaming in our heads, we must fight for truth. What is good, noble, true, right, pure, lovely, excellent, admirable, or praiseworthy about the situation (Phil 4:8)? About today? About our job as caregivers? *The power is in the focus.* We can't tell ourselves "stop thinking about the guilt, frustration, and pain," we must drown it out with truth and uplifting words. And we must remember that, as Christians with the indwelling Holy Spirit, we have the authority in Jesus' name to tell demons to flee. Stop behaving as though these negative thoughts are yours! They are not.

POSTLUDE

THE BIG H IS MUCH MORE POWERFUL THAN THE LITTLE D

As a child, I was taught to capitalize the "H" in "Him" and "His" when referring to God and His activities. Though some Bible translations no longer follow this practice, it serves as a reminder that God's power far exceeds our own and anything in His creation. His disruption of grammar rules is a small reflection of the immense power He wields.

In this book, I've intentionally written the devil with lowercase letters. We must always remember that the God with the "big H" is infinitely more powerful than the one with the "little d." We should never fear standing firm against the enemy.

If you get nothing further from this book, please internalize the following verses:

Ephesians 6:12 reminds us that our battle is "not against flesh and blood, but against the rulers, against the authorities, against the powers of this dark world and against the spiritual forces of evil in the heavenly realms." The battleground is in our mind, and the

Scripture verses that help me focus my mind on holy things are Galatians 5:22-23a and Philippians 4:8.

Galatians 5:22-23a: "But the fruit of the Spirit is love, joy, peace, patience, kindness, goodness, faithfulness, gentleness and self-control."

Philippians 4:8: "Finally brothers and sisters, whatever is true, whatever is noble, whatever is right, whatever is pure, whatever is lovely, whatever is admirable—if anything is excellent or praiseworthy—think about such things."

In Chapter 1, I spoke of "magic glasses" to help us see the spiritual world. I hope that this book has helped you "see" the spiritual warfare around you.

Always remember that the "Big H" is way bigger than the "little d," and with the indwelling Holy Spirit, you have the same authority as Jesus Himself to fight back against the enemy. Stand firm in truth, my friends.

A Final Note for Non-Christians

If you are still searching for meaning in this world apart from Jesus Christ, I understand. I used to be one of you. I spent 29 years running from Him, but then He came to me.

Whether you believe in Jesus or not, the devil still has dominion on planet Earth. He blinds us with pride so that we cannot see our sin or realize the need for a savior. He is the king of pride, and you are a pawn in his game.

Much of what people see as freedom is actually bondage. Bondage to fixed false beliefs. Bondage to pride. Bondage to a nonsensical notion that we can be our own gods or make our own truth. Truth is truth, whether we choose to believe it or not. The acceptance of truth brings freedom.

I ran away from the truth for 29 years, when truth came looking for me. Science was my religion back then, and I believed that, given enough time, science could explain everything. I believed I could use science to make life the way I wanted it. I could not see my own foolishness.

When science could not explain or fix my infertility, I had a crisis of faith. Science failed me. I could not escape the truth that there was another force at work in my fertility. What was now so precious to me was something I callously discarded when I aborted my first pregnancy 14 years before. Truth was staring me in the face. The devil tried to use guilt to keep me away from accepting Jesus, when Jesus was exactly what I needed.

All the spiritual warfare tactics discussed in this book depend on salvation, which provides the indwelling Holy Spirit. Do you want these strategies to work for you? If so, then you need to let go of your pride and unbelief and receive this gift today.

You could pray something like this:

Dear Jesus, I know that I am a sinner. I know that you came to die for my sins. I believe you defeated sin on the cross as a sacrifice for my sin and were raised from the dead. I accept your gift of salvation. Thank you, God, for saving me.

If you prayed that prayer, tell someone! Start visiting a grace-based, Bible-believing church to learn more. This is the only path to true freedom.

For color copies of this book's diagrams, discussion questions, study guides, and companion devotionals, please visit janethurleymd.com.

If you found this helpful or healing, I'd be grateful for an Amazon review.

References

Chapter 1: Defining the Problem

Anderson, N. (2000), Ch. 2: Finding Your Way in the World. *The bondage breaker.* (pp 29-42). Harvest House Publishers.

Chapter 2: Practicing Medicine Through a New Lens

Anderson, N. T., & Park, D. (2001). *The bondage breaker: Youth edition.* Harvest House Publishers.

Chapter 3: The Danger of Long-Term Bondage

Ephesians 6:12

Anderson, N. (2000), You don't have to live in the shadows. *The Bondage Breaker,* (pp 29-42). Harvest House Publishers.

Gillham, B. (1993). An "old man" in a new earthsuit. In *Lifetime guarantee: Making your Christian life work and what to do when it doesn't.* (pp. 71-86). Harvest House Publishers.

Schwartz, J. M., & Gladding, R. (2011). A new sense of self. In *You are not your brain: The 4-step solution for changing bad habits, ending unhealthy thinking, and taking control of your life.* Avery.

Chapter 4: Deception—"I'm Not Really Here"

Anderson, N. (2000), Ch. 11, The danger of deception. *The Bondage Breaker,* (p. 166). Harvest House Publishers.

Lewis, C. S. (1942). *The Screwtape Letters.* Geoffrey Bles.

Chapter 5: Temptation—"You Deserve Better"

1 Timothy 6:10

Philippians 4:12

1 John 2:16

Philippians 4:19

Philippians 4:11b-13

Anderson, N. (2000), Ch. 7, "Manipulating spirits." *The Bondage Breaker,* (p. 118-120). Harvest House Publishers.

Chapter 6: Condemnation—"You Are No Good"

The quote "Does it ever occur to you that nothing ever occurs to God" may have originated from Adrian Rogers. See: Rogers, A. (2008). *Adrianisms: The wit & wisdom of Adrian Rogers (Vol. 2).* Innovo Publishing.

Lowry, M., & Greene, B. (1991). *Mary, did you know?* [Song]. Word Music.

Matthew 25:14-30.

Chapter 7: The Hooks that Keep Us Stuck

Colossian 2:15

Romans 8:11

Anderson, N. (2000), Ch. 13, Steps to Freedom in Christ. *The Bondage Breaker,* (pp. 199-252). Harvest House Publishers.

West, M. (2012). *Forgiveness* [Song]. On Into the light. Sparrow Records.

Matthew 18:21-35

Anderson, N. T. (2013). "Healing emotional wounds from your past," *Victory over the darkness: Realize the power of your identity in Christ.* Bethany House Publishers.

Ephesians 4:27

Wills II, J. C., (2016). *Blessings through the seasons: A year of weekly devotions.* [Self-published].

Stone, D., & Gregory, D. (2000). "God's precious assets," *The rest of the gospel: When the partial gospel has worn you out,* (p. 113-120). Harvest House Publishers.

1 Corinthians 4:7

Galatians 5:22-23

Hebrews 8:12

Proverbs 16:18

Genesis 3:4b

Psalm 144:4

Ephesians 6:6

Anderson, N. (2000), Ch. 9, "Tempted to do it your way." *The Bondage Breaker,* (pp. 199-252). Harvest House Publishers.

Chapter 8: Getting a Handle on the Old Man

Galatians 5:22-23

Ephesians 2:6

Ephesians 2:19

Gillham, B. (1993). A "new man" in an old earthsuit. In *Lifetime guarantee: Making your Christian life work and what to do when it doesn't.* (pp. 71-86). Harvest House Publishers.

Gillham, B. (1993). "Handling Your Emotions" In *Lifetime guarantee: Making your Christian life work and what to do when it doesn't.* (pp. 143-156). Harvest House Publishers.

Chapter 9: Remembering Who You Really Are, and Who God Really Is

1 Corinthians 1:2

Camp, J. (2015). Same power [Song]. On I will follow. Sparrow Records; Stolen Pride LLC.

Galatians 5:22-23

1 Corinthians 13:4-8

Chapter 10: The Power of the Shield of Faith

Hebrews 11:1

Ephesians 6:13-17

Gillham, B. (1993). "Handling Your Emotions" In *Lifetime guarantee: Making your Christian life work and what to do when it doesn't.* (pp. 143-156). Harvest House Publishers.

As often attributed to Albert Einstein (though not verified in his writings): 'If I had an hour to solve a problem, I'd spend 55 minutes thinking about the problem and 5 minutes thinking about the solution.'

Chapter 11: Getting off the Hamster Wheel of Torment

Ephesians 6:16-17

Kendrick, A. (Director). (2015). War room [Film]. Provident Films; Affirm Films, Clip "Elizabeth Jordan sends the devil out of her house." https://www.youtube.com/watch?v=dkobFVAVlf8

Kendrick, A. (Director). (2015). War room [Film]. Provident Films; Affirm Films, Clip "My God is

powerful,"
https://www.youtube.com/watch?v=4j9zWQYYCLo

Galatians 5:22-23

Luke 22:31-34

Acts 5:1-10

Mark 2:14

Chapter 12: The Problem with "Righteous" Anger

Anderson, N. (2000), Ch. 7, "Manipulating spirits." *The Bondage Breaker,* (p. 118-120). Harvest House Publishers.

Matthew 21:12-13

Mark 11:15-18

Matthew 12:34

Luke 23:34

Berlinger, D. (Director). (2010). Amish grace [Film]. Lifetime Television.

Hebrews 12:15b

Hurley, J. (2024, November 14). 'Get coffee': FP leader's wisdom nurtures unity from conflict. *AAFP Voices.* American Academy of Family Physicians. https://www.aafp.org/news/blogs/aafp-voices/get-coffee.html

1 Kings 19:12b

Ephesians 6:15

Hurley, J. (2017, September 18). Talk where your feet are walking you. *Accepting the Maybe.* https://acceptingthemaybe.blogspot.com/2017/09/talk-where-your-feet-are-walking-you.html

Hurley, J. (2016, July 18). The search for integrity in uncomfortable places. *Accepting the Maybe.* https://acceptingthemaybe.blogspot.com/2016/07/the-search-for-integrity-in.html

Ecclesiastes 12:14

Ephesians 4:27

Philippians 4:8

Chapter 13: Anxiety

Matthew 6:25-34

Harvest House Publishers. Stone, D., & Gregory, D. (2000). *The rest of the gospel: When the partial gospel has worn you out* (p. 176). Harvest House Publishers.

Kendrick, A. (Director). (2011). *Courageous* [Film]. Provident Films; Affirm Films.

Anderson, N. T. (2013). "Healing emotional wounds from your past," *Victory over the darkness: Realize the power of your identity in Christ.* Bethany House Publishers.

Galatians 5:22a

Psalm 59:16-17, New Living Translation

Matthew 25:14-30

1 Kings Chapters 18 & 19

Chapter 14: Depression

Luke 4:1-8

Anderson, N. (2000), Ch. 7, "Manipulating spirits." *The Bondage Breaker,* (p. 118-120). Harvest House Publishers.

Matthew 14:22-32

Stone, D., & Gregory, D. (2000). "The Line," In *The rest of the gospel: When the partial gospel has worn you out,* (p. 27-34). Harvest House Publishers.

1 Kings 19:11-13

John 11:25

Kübler-Ross, E., & Kessler, D. (2005). On grief and grieving: Finding the meaning of grief through the five stages of loss. Scribner

Stone, D., & Gregory, D. (2000). "The gift of misery," In *The rest of the gospel: When the partial gospel has worn you out,* (p. 219-226). Harvest House Publishers.

Stone, D., & Gregory, D. (2000). "The single eye," In *The rest of the gospel: When the partial gospel has worn you out,* (p. 133-140). Harvest House Publishers.

Luke 4:9-12

Chapter 15: Healthy Eating

Philippians 4:8

Anderson, N. (2000), Ch. 7, "Manipulating spirits." *The Bondage Breaker,* (p. 118-120). Harvest House Publishers.

Ephesians 4:27

Hartwig, M. (n.d.). *Whole30.* Whole30, LLC. Retrieved November 25, 2025, from https://whole30.com/

Schmidt, Randy, "Karen Carpenter's tragic story. *The Guardian.* 10/23/2010. https://www.theguardian.com/books/2010/oct/24/karen-carpenter-anorexia-book-extract#:~:text=Karen%20Carpenter's%20velvet%20voice%20charmed,Schmidt%20tells%20the%20full%20story%E2%80%A6&text=The%20Carpenters%20were%20one%20of,selling%20more%20than%20100m%20records.

Bunnell, D., National Eating Disorders Association, Statistics, https://www.nationaleatingdisorders.org/statistics/, reviewed 11/9/2025.

Ephesians 6:12

Chapter 16: Exercise

Chapter 17: Healthcare Burnout

Merriam-Webster. (n.d.). Impostor syndrome. In *Merriam-Webster.com dictionary*. Retrieved November 25, 2025, from https://www.merriam-webster.com/dictionary/impostor%20syndrome

Landesman, P. (Director). (2013). Parkland [Film]. Exclusive Media; American Film Company; Millennium Entertainment.

Phil 4:8

Postlude: The Big H is Much More Powerful than the Little d

Ephesians 6:12

Galatians 5:22-23a

Philippians 4:8

About Kharis Publishing:

Kharis Publishing, an imprint of Kharis Media LLC, is a leading Christian and inspirational book publisher based in Aurora, Chicago metropolitan area, Illinois. Kharis' dual mission is to give voice to under-represented writers (including women and first-time authors) and equip orphans in developing countries with literacy tools. That is why, for each book sold, the publisher channels some of the proceeds into providing books and computers for orphanages in developing countries so that these kids may learn to read, dream, and grow. For a limited time, Kharis Publishing is accepting unsolicited queries for nonfiction (Christian, self-help, memoirs, business, health and wellness) from qualified leaders, professionals, pastors, and ministers.

Learn more at: https://kharispublishing.com/

www.ingramcontent.com/pod-product-compliance
Lightning Source LLC
La Vergne TN
LVHW010617100826
845148LV00014B/3008

* 9 7 8 1 6 3 7 4 6 6 9 0 2 *